MEALS ON THE MOVE

A CAMPSITE COOKING JOURNEY

KAREN WRIGHT

This book is dedicated to my two amazing daughters, Kit and Vanessa, the emerald and the ruby in my rusty crown, the lights of my life.

This edition first published in 2023 by Karen Wright

ISBN: 978-1-7394884-0-6

Designed by Mark Case at www.coversandcovers.com

Project management by Steve Rendle

Printed and bound in Malta

www.karenwrightbakes.co.uk
Follow Karen on Instagram @karenwrightbake

MEALS ON THE MOVE

A CAMPSITE COOKING JOURNEY

KAREN WRIGHT

CONTENTS

THE RECIPES

ENGLAND

Day 1   Dover   **1**

14   Guînes   Day 29-30

Day 27-28   Villeneuve-sur-Aisne   **13**

Day 2   Fontainebleau   **2**

Days 3-4   Gigny-sur-Saône   **3**

FRANCE

NOTE
Numbers in red circles on this map relate to the campsite locations listed on page 194.

Day 5-6   Vallon-Pont-d'Arc   **4**

– France - Italy - Switzerland –

ROUTE MAP
OUR 30-DAY JOURNEY

12   Saverne   Day 25-26

11   Colmar   Day 23-24

SWITZERLAND

10   Leukerbad   Day 21-22

9   Moniga del Garda   Day 18-20

8   Ca' Savio   Day 15-17

ITALY

Day 9-10   Sanremo   **6**

5   Volonne   Day 7-8

7   Lamporecchio   Day 11-14

'Sometimes the greatest meals
on vacation are the ones you find
when Plan A falls through!'

Anthony Bourdain

INTRODUCTION

When I was 12 years old, my parents bought their first caravan. Up until then we had always camped in tents. The caravan was second-hand and it cost £200. My mum let me count the money, all one-pound notes secured by an elastic band. I remember the feel of those notes and how thrilled I felt. We collected the caravan from a house near Eggborough, which was overlooked by the enormous cooling towers which dominate the area. I fell in love with that tiny caravan, it felt like a mini home, almost like living in a doll's house. I especially loved the kitchenette, and the seeds of a passion were sown.

Our first trip away was to Keswick in the Lake District. A few days before the trip I had found a stray dog. In those days it was normal to see dogs roaming around alone, but this dog was obviously abandoned. My parents let me keep her, we named her Sally and she came with us in the caravan on that holiday. On the very first morning we awoke to discover that we had stowaways, five new-born puppies!

Anything can and does happen in caravans and motorhomes. My caravan now doubles up as my prep kitchen when I work at food festivals. It's fantastic, as I have everything I need and I get all the many benefits of campsite life. Fresh air, changes of scenery, companionship, solitude – we all have our own reasons why we love camping, and for me the list is long.

This book is for anyone that loves to eat, drink, cook, travel, have a few laughs and would like to dine in style on a campsite. Welcome aboard!

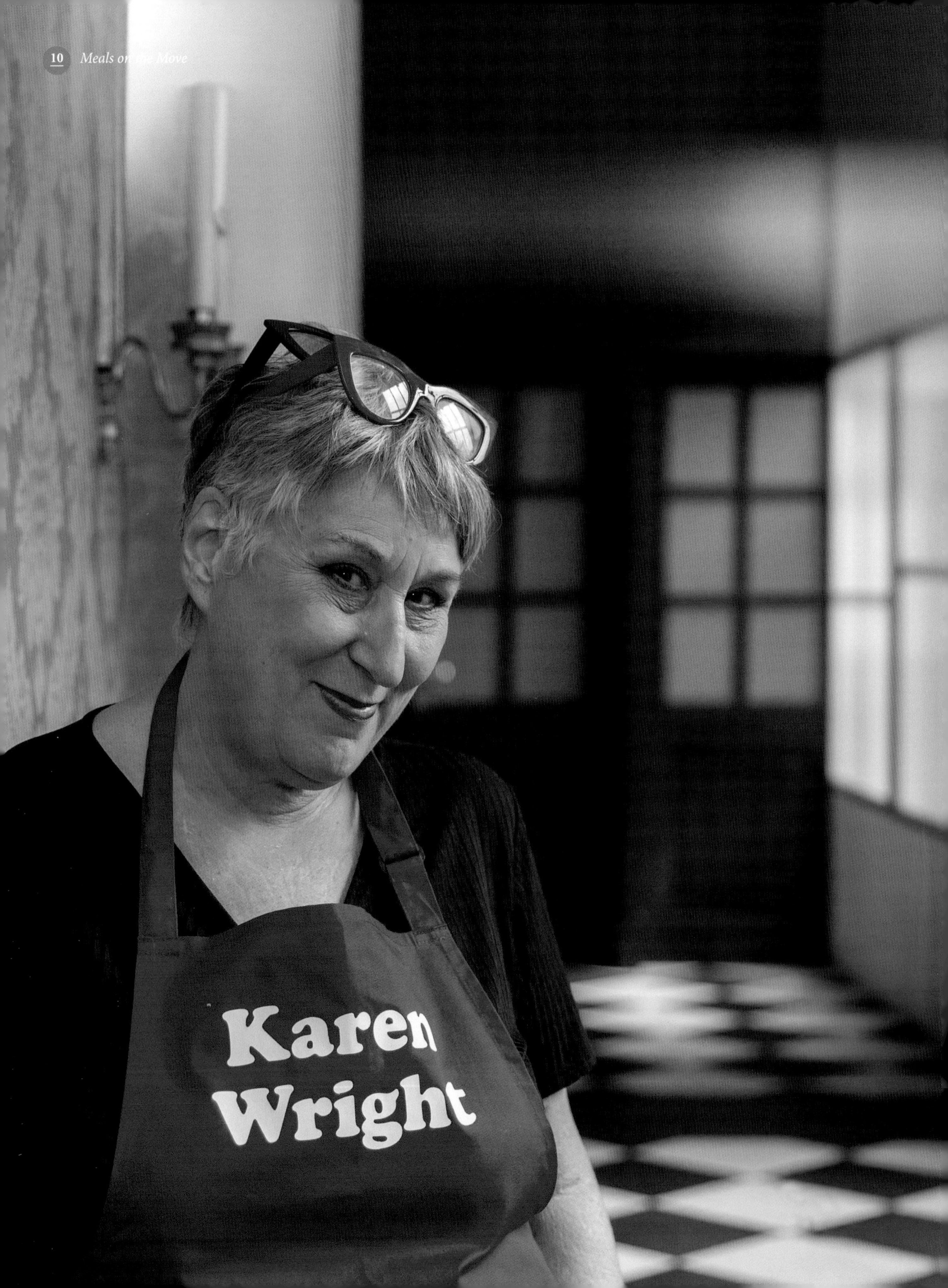
Karen
Wright

THE JOURNEY TO THIS BOOK

I'll start by telling you a little bit about me, my life, and my journey with food and travel. I was born in 1958 and at the time my parents were living with my older brother in Featherstone, West Yorkshire. My dad worked for the coal board as a joiner, and he was allocated a property that was to become our family home. The house was in a good location, but what set it apart from the norm was the type of house it was. It was hundreds of years old, we thought Elizabethan but we were never sure. It was in a bit of a state when my parents got the keys, but they had many skills between them and by the time I came along it was very comfortable. In fact, so much so that I thought we were quite 'posh'; it seemed very different to my grandparents' house down the road, which was a two-up, two-down terraced house with no inside toilet or bathroom and only a cold water tap in the scullery!

My mum always loved holidays, so my childhood memories are peppered with many trips away. We went to Butlin's several times, which I adored. My parents were both competitive, so we entered every contest we could. My dad had the most success winning the accolade of the knobbliest knees on the site! We also went camping, in tents at first and then in a caravan. The oddest tent we had was called a 'tentomatic', where the tent was part of a car roof rack. The idea was that you erected the tent whilst it was still attached to the top of the car, and then when it was all assembled and secured on the pitch the car was driven out from under it!

My parents' marriage was not made in heaven, and by the time I was 14 they had split up. Initially, I stayed with my dad and brother in the family home. I tried to keep up Mum's

housekeeping standards, but failed miserably. I became responsible for the cooking, which I didn't mind, as I had been well 'trained' by Mum. Mum had always baked each Sunday evening, and our cupboards were full of sponge cake, fruit cake and scones, enough to last us the week. She also taught me the basics of food preparation, so we ate well enough. Our meals were quite basic, mostly meat and vegetables, steamed fish, cottage pie, liver and onions, but I already enjoyed messing around in the kitchen.

Time moved on and so did I. I got a job in a bank when I was 16, and I also got married! I was 16, with a job, a husband and a house, which seems extraordinary looking back. Financially, things were very tight, and cracks soon started to appear in our relationship. We had a falling out one day which culminated in me moving to Mum's for the weekend to allow breathing

space for us both. In fact, I never went back, and we ended our marriage amicably enough and both went our separate ways.

Around this time, one of my friends, Caroline, was encouraging me and another friend, Karen, to save up some money so that we could go on holiday together to Greece. We saved enough, and after flying to Athens, we boarded a boat to a small island called Spetses. This trip heralded another big change for me. Suffice it to say, Cupid had his eye on me and decided to shoot an arrow in my direction. I began a love affair with both a Greek and Greece, that was very on and off for a few years. I eventually sold my house and went to work on the island. I had a few jobs there, but the most random was becoming a gamekeeper's assistant for Stavros Niarchos, the shipping magnate and arch enemy of Aristotle Onassis.

In the early '80s, the food on the island was very similar in all the tavernas during the tourist season. All the menus featured moussaka of course, as well as stuffed tomatoes and aubergines, Greek salads, roast chicken, and green beans. Outside of the season, the tavernas served more local specialities. My two favourites, even to this day, are briam, an oven-baked dish of potatoes and vegetables, and gigantes plaka, which is a simple but scrumptious dish of giant beans

in tomato sauce. Not all of the meals were to my taste though. One old lady that I was friendly with invited me into her house for lunch one day – she sat me down at a huge table covered with an oilcloth and placed a steaming bowl of soup in front of me, complete with fish heads and octopus tentacles!

At this time, it was common to see old women, often dressed in black, carrying trays of food to the baker's shop. This is when I discovered that many Greek homes did not have an oven, so anything that needed baking was taken to the baker's and cooked in their giant ovens after they had finished making the bread for the day. I learned a great deal from my time on Spetses, and remember it all with great affection.

My time in Greece came to an end when I discovered I was expecting a baby, and I decided to come back to the UK. The birth of my first daughter, Katharine, was the best day of my life thus far, and I was the happiest I had ever been. The years passed, and Katharine and I were a gang of two for long enough. When she was seven, I married John.

The back story for John and I is a funny one. He was my uncle's best friend, and I first clapped eyes on him when I was seven, at my maternal grandmother's house – he would have

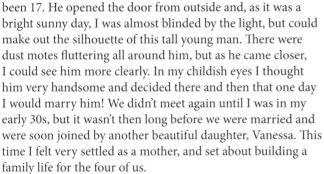

been 17. He opened the door from outside and, as it was a bright sunny day, I was almost blinded by the light, but could make out the silhouette of this tall young man. There were dust motes fluttering all around him, but as he came closer, I could see him more clearly. In my childish eyes I thought him very handsome and decided there and then that one day I would marry him! We didn't meet again until I was in my early 30s, but it wasn't then long before we were married and were soon joined by another beautiful daughter, Vanessa. This time I felt very settled as a mother, and set about building a family life for the four of us.

Now I really wanted to get into the groove of domesticity, and I took great satisfaction from cooking for us. John came into the marriage with very traditional views on meals – meat and two veg or anything with chips was his idea of a good dish. He didn't eat rice, and still doesn't, unless it is rice pudding! Back then he didn't eat pasta or pizza, so I was stuck with potatoes! Things have moved on, and I tease him now, saying he is the best-fed man on our housing estate, as I'm always testing out so many recipes and new ideas for dishes.

We went on holiday as often as we could, and over the years we had caravans, tents and motorhomes. They were all old,

but we had good times all the same. Mine and John's first trip together was in 1989. We had been courting for just a few months when he suggested a camping trip to the French Alps. We headed off to Chamonix and had a few glorious days until the heavens opened. Being in a very small dome tent, we were soon a bit soggy and fed up, so we moved to find the sun. We found the sun in the wonderful Ardèche Gorges. We returned home via the Loire valley, and we hit a heatwave. This time, the dome tent was scorching hot, and we were constantly on the lookout for shade. Pitched by the river at Amboise, I remember standing in the shower block, pulling the chain on an antiquated shower and being doused in icy-cold water, which felt fabulous. Even more fabulous was the moment when I came out and was walking back to the tent, and saw a flotilla of hot air balloons floating by. What a glorious sight.

In 2002 we bought a holiday home in France and then my love story with the country intensified. We enjoyed almost 20 years visiting as often as we could. The house needed a lot of work, so we decided to move there for a year. Vanessa even went to the local secondary school while we completed the renovations. The best part of owning the holiday home in France was the parties. We became friends with other expats in the area, as well as our French neighbours, so when the

weather forecast was good, I would send out an invitation to come over for a BBQ or just nibbles and drinks. It was a wonderful place for socialising. We had a swimming pool which, although the water was always perishing cold, was pretty to sit around with friends.

Once a year there was a fête in the village, and we would invite family and friends to visit so they could enjoy some local life. We would divide into small teams to do the cooking for the evening meals, each team taking a turn. We had some good laughs; the team members were picked out of a hat so you might be on a lucky team with foodie types, or you might be on a team with the folk that normally just do the washing-up. While the on-duty team cooked, everyone else would relax with a drink, or maybe have a ping-pong tournament. As the evening wore on, it was quite usual for someone to end up in the pool! When I was on *The Great British Bake Off*, the first Showstopper Challenge was to create a huge biscuit selfie with a back-story related to the contestant. Mine was all about that holiday home!

Over these years, food and cooking became very important to me, and from time to time I played with the idea of developing my interest into a business. However, I didn't feel I had the resources or the qualifications, so I just continued to potter in the kitchen. Yet, at family gatherings I came into my own, and was always cooking mountains of food to bring to the table. Even now you can look in my freezer and inevitably you will find a quiche, or some sausage rolls, that I have made ready to bring out at a moment's notice should unexpected company arrive, or should we be invited somewhere for a get-together. If it is my turn to host, I love to get pen and paper out to plan my menu and ingredient lists – the only shopping I enjoy is grocery shopping!

So how did I get from enjoying cooking for friends and taking family holidays abroad to writing this book? Well, all my life, every so often when my instincts are twitching, I act. There is a trendy term for it now, it is called taking 'instinctive

action'. I just always thought it was time for a change, time to shake things up a bit, but now we know – I was allowing my intuition to guide me in the direction I was to go. Let me give you a few examples where I followed my intuition, leading to exciting things happening as a result.

As I've mentioned, we used to have a holiday home in France, but the story behind how we came to own it is a great example of taking instinctive action. It was the early 2000s, and we were thinking about buying a holiday home. We went for a single day to view houses, just to get a feel for the idea. We viewed four properties: the first two I didn't like, the third was out of our budget, but the fourth… well, it just was calling my name from every corner, nook and cranny! We signed on the dotted line then and there. This house was the setting for so many lovely holidays and some great memories with family and friends were made there.

A few years later, one of my daughters started working in France for a holiday company. She told me about jobs that were being done by people of my age – I think I was just 50. I applied, along with John, and within weeks we were up and away and working on a campsite in Burgundy. We worked seven seasons in total, living all over France looking after mobile homes and tents. We had the time of our lives!

As I approached my 60th birthday, my daughter sent me the link to apply for *The Great British Bake Off*. I had been decorating quite a few cakes for birthdays, and she thought I was quite good. I opened the application form, looked at the questions and was just about to close my laptop and dismiss the idea because I could see that I had never done any of the things they were asking for. I had only ever made Victoria sponge cake, scones, and shortcrust pastry. All those different cakes, pastries, breads, and fillings were just not part of my baking repertoire! However, something happened; that niggling voice was telling me something. I listened, as it said: 'How hard can it be to teach yourself; you have two months

before the application deadline.' I jumped up and set to work in the kitchen! I set about baking my way onto the show. I was eager and really got stuck in, making and photographing the bakes and ticking the boxes on the application as I went along. There were more than 25,000 applicants that year, all trying to win one of the 12 places on the iconic show. I was one of the 12!

When I left the show at the halfway mark, a strange thing – almost a premonition – occurred. I was being interviewed on camera for my exit from the show, and I was a bit teary. When they asked me what I was planning to do next, I stretched my arm out towards the camera and said: 'No more baking for a while, I am going away in my caravan!' I didn't have any plans in place, nor had I even thought about the caravan, but those words came out in a rush. When I returned that evening to the hotel, I was relaxing and scrolling through social media. I saw one of the managers from my old camping-job days asking if anyone was available at short notice to go to France to clean 20 mobile homes. I got in touch there and then. I asked how soon she needed someone; her answer was 'tomorrow'. I responded: 'Well I can't do tomorrow, but I can do the next

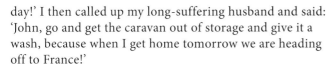

day!' I then called up my long-suffering husband and said: 'John, go and get the caravan out of storage and give it a wash, because when I get home tomorrow we are heading off to France!'

Since *The Great British Bake Off* I have discovered so much more about myself than I ever knew before. I am excited to expand my horizons and do many more things. I like to step up to the plate, jump outside the box and out of my comfort zone, and I listen and continue to act when intuition calls. So many people have asked if I would write a book. They do say everyone has at least one book in them, and this is mine. I am listening to that call, that intuition, that says, 'If not now, when?'

I didn't want to write a traditional recipe book, nor a baking book, as I am still on a baking learning curve. However, I do love to cook. I have always been keen on feeding people and learning about new ingredients and the culture of food. I also love to holiday in either a caravan or a motorhome and enjoy creating delicious meals inspired by wherever I am holidaying at the time. This book combines these two passions to show how you can make amazing meals, quickly and easily, in your caravan, motorhome, or tent!

However, it hasn't always been like this. When I was a child on camping holidays, there was no real finesse or enjoyment involved in creating a meal. My mum would pack up the car full of packets and tins, quite often things that we would never eat at home, like tinned minced steak or tinned Irish stew. I remember to this day the congealed rim of white fat that clung to the top of the tin once it had been opened. My mum was a decent cook, and at home we only ate fresh food cooked from scratch, but this wasn't the case for our holidays. When I grew up and had a family of my own, for long enough I followed suit. Although I must say, I never did buy that Irish stew – I drew a line at that! I would buy 'cook in sauce' jars and tins of curry or chilli for example, and we enjoyed them well enough and didn't feel hungry, but neither was there any style, and certainly no anticipation of a fantastic lunch or evening meal.

Finally, I wondered why it is that when we holiday in a caravan or a motorhome, we don't eat half as well as we do at home? Surely part of the enjoyment of a holiday is to dine well, like you would in a hotel, to anticipate a delicious meal and enjoy some extra holiday treats. The seeds of an idea were planted then for this book! How hard would it be to develop

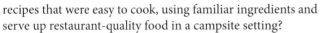

recipes that were easy to cook, using familiar ingredients and serve up restaurant-quality food in a campsite setting?

This book covers the 30 days I took out of my regular life to drive through to France, Italy and Switzerland with my husband, John, on a lovely long touring holiday. Before I set off, I worked on the 30 recipes that appear in this book. They are all my twists on classic French, Italian and Swiss dishes. I have worked on them to make them campsite friendly but have kept them as authentic as possible. Most are authentic to the region we were staying in at the time, but certainly to the country. Some are main meals; some are snacks or light lunches. Of course, on holiday, eating out is an occasional must too, as is having a good old barbecue and a few beers – there is time for everything and everything has its time.

Speaking of baking, I have baked in my caravan in the past, but on this trip, I decided against it. With so many wonderful patisseries, boulangeries and artisanal markets to buy exquisite treats from in the countries we were visiting, it would have been folly not to buy from them and take some time to relax – it was a holiday for me, after all.

I also wanted my book to be real, nothing plastic or glossy, which is why I decided to include a 'Dear Diary' section covering every day of the trip, warts and all. So, my book is part travel blog, part cookbook, part diary and hopefully part funny and inspirational too. So come on, let's get out of the kitchen and rattle some pots and pans. Grab your passport, and let's go on a road trip, let's make some meals on the move. Join me, and let's cook my way on the highway!

BEFORE WE SET OFF

Owning a caravan or motorhome has probably never been as popular as it is right now. The flexibility it offers for holidays is fantastic. Go where you like, when you like, up sticks if the weather is poor and chase the sun – you can really experience the freedom to roam. Many people have even made it a lifestyle change, and live in their leisure vehicle full-time. There are so many television programmes being broadcast that follow celebrities around in their motorhomes, it certainly whets the appetite and encourages us to give it a try. It can be really easy and fun to cook food to enjoy on the campsite. With just some basic equipment and some simple ingredients, you can whip up great food for you, your friends and family, without breaking the bank, or even a sweat!

This book includes 30 delicious recipes (all serving two, unless stated otherwise) that I hope all readers will enjoy. Every recipe can be cooked on a hob using either one or two pans. I have written the ingredient quantities as far as possible, using handfuls, knobs or splashes, as I don't carry weighing scales with me. I do carry measuring cups, a measuring jug and a set of spoons (a list of suggested equipment is given on pages 22–23). The recipes are all intended to be quick to make and should all be ready within 30 minutes, so we don't empty our gas bottles or use too much electricity! Although, I do enjoy cooking slowly, sitting outside in the early evening, with a glass of wine, chopping my vegetables and soaking up the fresh air and the atmosphere. I have only used ingredients or suggested alternatives that are easily sourced, and there's a list of recommended ingredients to keep in stock throughout a trip on the right.

All the recipes have been tested by friends, family and my caravan and motorhome club pals, but I urge everyone to adapt the ingredients and swap out anything they don't fancy. With cooking there are few hard and fast rules!

Ingredients

I have included a list of the ingredients that I often carry with me. This list isn't exhaustive but most of the items listed are used for recipes in this book. However, it is important to check what foods you cannot take with you internationally. For example, there are rules on which meat and milk products can be taken into EU countries. Please check the advice on local laws and customs on the UK government's foreign-travel advice website for the country you are visiting for more information (https://www.gov.uk/foreign-travel-advice).

Although I take some things with me from home, as we approach a campsite I will call in at the shops, market or supermarket to pick up fresh items for the next couple of days. I carry a working quantity of store-cupboard ingredients with me, including the makings of at least one complete meal in case of emergency or hunger strikes! My tuna pasta recipe on page 96 is ideal for this, delicious too!

Store-cupboard Staples
- Olive oil
- Chilli flakes
- Oregano
- Thyme
- Smoked paprika
- Garlic purée
- Mustard/s
- Salt and pepper
- Ketchup
- Tomato purée
- Worcestershire sauce
  (works in lieu of anchovies)
- Capers
- Black olives
- Stock cubes/pots
- Vinegars
- Breadcrumbs
- Tinned tomatoes
- Passata
- Tinned tuna
- Sundried tomatoes
- Longlife/UHT milk and cream
- Plain flour
- Pasta
- Tortilla wraps
- Bread
- Biscuits
- Cereal
- Sugar
- Tea
- Coffee
- Red wine
- Onions
- Potatoes
- Eggs

Chilled Items
- Milk
- Cheese
  (cheddar and parmesan)
- Bacon
- Butter
- White wine
- Beer

Individual preferences vary, and everyone will adapt the list to suit themselves. Remember that many things can be swapped out and alternatives used. This is especially so with dried herbs and spices. For example, Herbes de Provence, Italian mixed herbs and oregano all tick the same box for me, so I would just choose one, not take one of each. Chillies can be dried, in a purée or in a little jar, or of course you may buy fresh, but in terms of trying to pack light just having one would work. A can of mixed beans can be swapped for cannellini or borlotti beans – beans are beans in my book, at a push even good old baked beans will fit many recipes. I do urge everyone to be creative and throw in a few curveballs now and then. This is the way recipes evolve and it can be great fun putting your own stamp on a dish!

Measurements

Cooking is not like baking, it is not an exact science, there are no rules. You can add and subtract as you feel inclined. Baking is more exact, and the rules rule in the kitchen. You won't find any baking recipes in this book! Neither will you find the need for a set of scales. Being on holiday should be more about loosening your stays, not just your underwear, but your attitude to cooking. My instructions include things like, 'a handful of this', 'a splash of that', 'a knob of the other'. I use measuring spoons and a small measuring jug, but I also use my eyes, my hands and my imagination to gauge quantities. I might say use eight mushrooms, but if you only have six, use six, and if you have nine, use nine – don't leave a mushroom all alone in the world! You get my drift? Good!

The cases when I do mention weights in grams would be where you would see the weight on a pack of, say, sausages, or a can of tomatoes or a jar of something. Then, using the eyeball technique, you would calculate what you need to use. It's a great technique to master, the old eyeball one!

Equipment

It is very easy to get excited and carried away when buying equipment for your leisure vehicle. I know this myself – I don't enjoy shopping, apart for ingredients of course, but I do love buying things for the van. It is like a little home on wheels,

and we are all keen to set it up with all the home comforts. I have learned from experience that I always pack too much stuff – clothes, shoes, food, pots and pans. So now I try to be very disciplined and keep to a bare minimum. Let's face it – if you are short of something, you can usually borrow or buy it on your trip. It is also important to remember that there is a maximum towing capacity for caravans, and a maximum payload for motorhomes, and you must not exceed this. Experience will tell you what is right for your set-up, but I have included a list of my basics.

Cooking-wise, I am working on the assumption that not everyone has an oven in their unit. So, the recipes in this book rely on hobs alone. This will work for anyone who is camping under canvas too, all-inclusive recipes here! I also don't include any aids like slow cookers, air-fryers or pressure-cookers for the same reason. Not everyone has them, and they are bulky, so they eat into storage space.

The recipes are as minimalistic as possible. Many use just one pan, or occasionally two. For most recipes I use a large frying pan with a lid. Nesting sets of bowls and pans are the way forward too, as they help save space. This is my list of cooking equipment that I like to take with me:

- Nesting set of pans with detachable handle/grip
- Non-stick frying pan
- Large/deep frying pan with lid
- Nesting mixing bowls/colander
- Balloon whisk
- Wooden spoon
- Silicone spatula
- Fish slice/slotted spoon set
- Set of measuring spoons
- Measuring jug marked with cups and millilitres measurements
- Set of metal skewers *(for use on the barbecue)*
- Two chopping boards *(one for meat and one for everything else)*
- Melamine serving platter
- Scissors
- Veg knife/bread knife/general knife
- Corkscrew/bottle opener
- Can opener
- Small, boxed cheese grater
- Cutlery set
- Melamine plates and cups
- Plastic glasses
- Tea towels/dishcloths/sponges
- Kettle
- Cling film/tinfoil
- Matches or lighter
- Gas barbecue
- Barbecue tongs
- Set of nesting food boxes *(Tupperware style)*
- Plastic tablecloth for outside

Many of these items can serve two purposes. The mixing bowls can become salad or fruit bowls for example. I haven't included a vegetable peeler, as I don't use one very often, so you may want to tailor the list to your own requirements.

Shopping

On holidays, I try to shop every day or every second day. Access to supermarkets can be a pain if your unit is a motorhome or campervan, as upping sticks to go and buy groceries can be a major operation. I do plan my menu a couple of days ahead for this reason. In fact, for this trip, I knew exactly what I was cooking every day before I even set off from Yorkshire, which may reduce spontaneity but

adds to the ease of the day. For example, as we drove towards Burgundy, I stopped off just before we checked into the campsite at the nearest supermarket and picked up two days' worth of fresh ingredients for the mushroom Bourguignon and the coq au vin I intended to cook. Remember though, it's OK if you can't get all the fresh ingredients on the list for a particular recipe, as necessity is the mother of invention!

Food Preparation

It should be possible to cook all the recipes in 30 minutes or less. This is only to save energy – gas or electricity. I like to linger longer when cooking, but it is up to you if you want to beat the clock.

Throughout the recipes, there are techniques designed to speed things up. First, I prep my ingredients before I start to cook anything, including peeling and chopping. In my recipes, I often use words like, 'finely dice' or 'chop into small chunks' – this is to enable some ingredients, like carrots, to cook more quickly. If I say chop in halves or thickly slice, this will be to keep some texture in the dish, with mushrooms for example. Otherwise, they wilt to nothing, and texture and bite is lost.

Sometimes the recipe will note to cook potatoes either fully or par-boil beforehand. This is for the same reason, as cooking them can hold things up otherwise.

Remember though, the anticipation of anything is part of the joy, and for me that is especially the case with food. Savour the smells and the sounds of your dish as it cooks, relax and enjoy the moment. When dishing up the final result, keep in mind the saying 'we eat with our eyes'. Take care with how you plate up your meal, as attractively presented food will spike your taste buds and get that restaurant vibe buzzing around your table.

Cooking Chicken

Some of my recipes include boneless and skinless chicken thighs – being 'off' the bone reduces cooking time. However, if you can't purchase boneless thighs, then chicken breast can be used, or thighs on the bone. If chicken is on the bone, it will require longer cooking times and careful checking that the meat is cooked and no pink is visible.

Cooking Pasta

As many of the recipes were cooked during our time in Italy, and include pasta, I thought I'd give some tips on cooking perfect pasta.

- Always boil water in the largest pan you have and add a tablespoon of salt.

- If the pasta is in a small pan, it cannot swirl around and it becomes very gluey.

- Salt is essential to good flavour, and remember most of it will be drained away. Don't rinse your cooked pasta.

- Don't be tempted to add oil to the water, as this just prevents the sauce sticking to the pasta.

- Always reserve a cupful of the pasta water to add to the sauce, as it will create a great glossy emulsion.

- Undercook the pasta for two minutes from the time given on the pack instructions. Lift the pasta out and into the sauce, then continue to cook for two minutes in the sauce. It should still be 'al dente', which means if you bite a strand, it still has a little resistance.

- For measuring spaghetti, that hole in the middle of a pasta lifter is meant to measure one portion.

- If you cook too much pasta, don't worry, pop it in the fridge and it makes a great breakfast the next day. (Unless you are my cousin Janet who won't eat anything cold that was previously hot!)

Now, let's get cooking…

– Day 1 –
DOVER,
KENT

was, hearing the dawn chorus and then trying out all the 'get to sleep quick' tricks in my repertoire, but alas, zero winks were to be had. Anyway, it was finally time to get up, get showered, do a few final checks on passports, cash, paperwork and medication, and close the house down for a month. I have even defrosted both of my fridges and freezers, and the electricity is very firmly in the off position – make what you will of that Mr. Smart Meter!

After filling the motorhome with fuel, we were off. We know this leg of our journey like the back of our hands – I have lost count of the times we have bombed off from Wakefield to Dover via the A1. The weather was as dull as dishwater and chilly too, which was a surprise after the heatwave of the last few days. An uneventful journey, and even the liquorice allsorts were a bit lacklustre, but then they were rip-offs rather than the real deal, so I should have expected that. Dull sweets and grey skies could not dampen our enthusiasm though, and we were happily singing along to playlists that I had managed to Bluetooth to the motorhome stereo – I am learning so many new skills these days it's untrue.

Day one of the much-awaited motorhome trip to France, Italy and Switzerland finally dawned. I wonder why it is that when you need a good night's sleep to set you up for the next day, you never get one! I was tossing and turning all last night, looking to see what time it

As we approached the campsite that we are staying at tonight – our last one in the UK for a while – the silly sat-nav took us down some winding country roads, single-track most of the time. I was sitting on the edge of my seat hoping and praying that another big vehicle would not come towards us. Prayers answered, we managed to navigate to the campsite without incident. We checked in and were allocated a 'ferry pitch', as we are leaving early-doors in the morning to head off to the port to catch our ferry. The pitch is close to the exit, so hopefully we won't disturb any of the other guests.

We hooked up to the electricity and put the kettle on. I bought a groovy little silicone kettle which collapses into itself when not in use – very cool! After we'd had a cuppa, I had a quick look at the road map for tomorrow's journey. I bought John a fancy sat-nav last Christmas, but it's so fancy we haven't quite figured out how to use it yet. Anyway, I quite like a map on my lap as we drive along. We are heading down to a campsite close to Fontainebleau, south of Paris tomorrow. It looks quite straightforward, and we have been there before, but of course anything can and often does go a bit belly-up, so I am trying to prepare myself for all eventualities.

My tummy started rumbling at about five o'clock and I realised it had been hours since we ate anything. Hurrah, time to test out recipe number one! As it was our last meal in the UK for a month, I thought I would treat John to a last British supper that he would definitely like. The thing with him is, he really isn't keen on pasta, and he will not eat rice (unless it's a pudding), so that pretty much leaves us with spuds. When we hit Italy of course, lots of my recipes include pasta, so I thought we would have one last go with something akin to chips. In France, steak frites is on pretty much every menu, so my recipe is a nod to that – a lovely juicy (hopefully not tough) steak with sautéed potatoes and peppercorn sauce.

I brought the ingredients for this with me, as it was easier than trying to second-guess the shopping locally and we have

a massive fridge/freezer in the motorhome. I decided to cook indoors tonight, as it was still grey and chilly outside and we were comfy and happy inside. We have a four-ring hob, a grill and a big oven in the motorhome, which is amazing and I am very chuffed with it. I cooked the meal as per my recipe and

made a few minor amendments, then we sat down to enjoy. I gave myself a pat on the back, as it was all spot-on and very quick and easy, which is exactly as it should be. We cracked open a bottle of wine, of course, and we polished that off quick sticks. John was telling me there is a Battle of Britain memorial nearby and, if we had more time, we would have gone to see it. Always the case when you are moving on, and I shall make a note of it as something to do the next time we are down here. Tomorrow's menu at Fontainebleau is French onion soup, so before bed I decided to peel and slice the onions, as I have a sneaky feeling the drive tomorrow may be longer than I initially thought, and if that job is already done I will be ahead of my own game.

I decided to set a few intentions for the trip, so before we lowered the very state-of-the-art bed down from the ceiling – I kid you not! – I made a list. First-up was to try to swim every day. Second is to remember to practise gratitude. Third is to try to stay in the moment and enjoy everything as it unfurls, and not to be champing at the bit to be in the next place or do the next thing. The last thing is to try not to be irritated with John and be kinder. John is a bit more forgetful these days, and that brings challenges for us both. He is not a bad old stick, and I am determined to be better around him.

Time to lower the bed and get some good-quality winks. Big day tomorrow, and the excitement is bubbling. Time to say bye to Britain and bonjour to France!

– Day 1 Recipe –

STEAK AND SAUTÉED POTATOES WITH PEPPERCORN SAUCE

Steak frites is served everywhere in France, but it likely originates from the north of France, close to Belgium. It is simple to prepare and delicious. Frites (which are what we call chips or French fries in the UK) are not easy to make in caravans or motorhomes, and certainly not tents, unless you have a new-fangled air fryer with you. Sautéed potatoes on the other hand are very easy and just as scrumptious! A word of advice: the potatoes need to be cooked and chilled beforehand to ensure they don't break up when they are sautéed.

Ingredients (serves 2)

Sautéed potatoes

- Cold cooked potatoes (*2 large baking-sized potatoes, cut into 1cm-thick slices*)
- 2 tablespoons olive oil
- Grind of sea salt
- Squeeze of lemon juice

Steak

- Sirloin steaks (*faux filet*) at room temperature
- 2 tablespoons cognac or 100ml white wine
- 100ml beef stock (*stock cube/pot*)
- 1 teaspoon black peppercorns
- Grind of pepper
- 100ml cream
- Parsley garnish

Method

In a large frying pan, heat the oil and sauté the potato slices over a moderate heat. It is important not to crowd the pan. Cook for about 15 minutes, or until starting to become golden brown. Season well with salt, and serve with a squeeze of lemon juice.

Prepare the steak by brushing or rubbing with oil. Heat a griddle or frying pan for a couple of minutes and then place the steaks into it. Cook the steaks on one side for about five minutes, and then turn and cook the other side. The cooking time depends on how you like your steak – medium-rare is approximately four minutes on each side, depending on the thickness of the meat. Once cooked, it is very important to rest the steak for five minutes off the heat, on a plate covered loosely with foil. This allows the meat to relax and the juices to settle.

To make the sauce, pour the stock, white wine/cognac and the peppercorns into the pan with the steak juices. Bring to a rapid boil and keep on the boil for a few minutes to reduce the volume, then pour in the cream and an extra grind of pepper. Continue to cook for a couple of minutes to thicken the sauce.

When the steak is rested, plate up with the sautéed potatoes, garnish with the parsley if you wish, and serve the sauce on the side.

The oldest form
of theatre is the
dinner table.

Michael J Fox

France. How do I love her? Let me count the ways...

I love her sights, I love her sounds, I love her smell. I love her open roads. I love her bustling streets. I love her snowcapped mountains, her sandy beaches.

I love her verdant gorges and her open plains. I love her shuttered windows and her tolling bells. I love her slight aloofness, like a cat, I think, of all things, I love that!

I was 14 when I first visited France, and I flew to Paris with my mum. My first impression when we were travelling by coach from the airport into the city was of those long, straight boulevards lined with plane trees. Everything looked, and certainly sounded, very different to back home in Yorkshire. Mum thought I could speak the language, as I had lessons at school and had won a prize for reciting a French poem. She was disappointed that I wouldn't pipe up in the shops and on the metro. Struck by teenage awkwardness, I couldn't bring myself to utter a word!

As an adult, I have travelled in France many times. For holidays, when our children were small, we camped, motorhomed and caravanned in many of the popular tourist areas. We started with the French Alps, Ardèche, Loire and Dordogne, and moved on over the years to Brittany, Normandy, Vendée, Biarritz and the Mediterranean coast. During our years working in France in the camping industry, we were based first in Burgundy, then the Côte d'Azur, the Loire, Dordogne and Picardy. We also visited sites in Switzerland, Luxembourg and Germany.

Many people have asked what I love about France, and I usually answer 'everything'. France is a big country. All the regions offer differences, but similarities too. I love how, as you drive along from region to region, the landscape changes, subtly sometimes and other times with drama. The rooftops and churches change in style and colour, and little by little you start to feel a change in vibration. Slight nuances that a change in geography, and in temperature, can bring to a place.

As I journey through France on this trip, I will be visiting some places that I have been before. I look forward to that, but I will also be travelling to pastures new. On the journey back home, I will find myself in the east of the country, almost touching Germany and Belgium. That is very exciting – new sights, sounds and tastes to be discovered. On the subject of taste, France has a reputation for having fantastic food. Many top chefs have trained in France. There are hundreds of dishes to master. Every region seems to have its own specialities, but then you can find croque messieurs and steak frites in cafés everywhere. I have never dined in any top restaurants in France, but I have had many a fantastic dinner in a tucked-away brasserie or a Relais Routier truckers' café.

Even the schools in France take the food and menus very seriously. Two hours is allocated for a three-course school lunch. The menu is posted up outside the school for all to see. Those children have the most wonderful diets. Always a salad to start, fish or meat for main and a little dessert and cheese to finish, with bread on the table, of course, and a carafe of water.

I was once at a big party where there were both French and English children. The French children ignored all the crisps and salty nibbles on offer, and loaded their plates with cherry tomatoes, cucumber and lettuce. I was fascinated.

Everything stops for lunch in France. If you happen to be in one of the big supermarkets that have a restaurant, you may struggle to find a free table between 12 noon and 2pm. They are full. The choices are spectacular. The salad bar, the 'plats', the grills, the fish, the cheese boards, the desserts. It really is a sight to behold, and very good value. I recommend giving it a try! It is important to remember that some shops close at lunchtime, so make sure you check the opening hours before you set out with your shopping list.

I discovered first-hand that French people generally have their main meal at lunchtime. We had a neighbour in our French village, Dee Dee, that we loved dearly. She cooked herself a meal every lunchtime, sometimes pasta or maybe chicken. She varied it every day with fresh vegetables from her garden and a little sauce on the side. She sat at the kitchen table with a baguette she bought every morning from the boulangerie, and enjoyed her meal. I was always intrigued to see what she was cooking each day.

This same neighbour introduced us to the etiquette of the 'apéro' (short for apéritif). In France it is common to invite friends for an 'apéro' in the early evening, which typically involves an alcoholic drink and a nibble of something savoury. She would invite us to come to her kitchen at about 6pm. On the table would be two or three bottles of spirits. Typically, she would have pastis, whisky and a little sweet wine for herself. She would pile plates with crackers or nuts, and she would pour the drinks – great big measures, often with no mixers, just a cube of ice. Conversation followed, all in French, which was tricky, but became easier after another great big measure of booze. After about an hour it would be time to go. We often never managed to make our evening meal thanks to the hospitality of Dee Dee, as we were too tipsy!

Bon Route!

– Day 2 –
FONTAINEBLEAU,
ÎLE-DE-FRANCE

What a day. Like the curate's egg, it's been good in parts, but it has also been a bit white-knuckle. We decided to set an alarm and try to catch an earlier ferry. The alarm went off at 5:30am, but I had been waiting for it to sing to me for ages. Another night's sleep interrupted by my busy brain. Anyway, we hightailed off to Dover ferry port and by the skin of our teeth managed to catch the earlier sailing.

I really like a cross-Channel ferry; the anticipation is usually better than the reality, including today's full-English breakfast that we both ate. It looked fine, and it was, but by the time

we'd picked up a hot drink, paid for it and found a seat it was quite cold. I should have known better, but anyway it charged us up for the day and really that is what we needed. When we docked at Calais the weather was as grey as smoke and quite chilly. By the time we had driven half an hour down the coast it was perking up, and very soon after it was scorching.

The roads were quiet, and we bombed along and hardly saw another vehicle – until we hit the outskirts of Paris and then it was hectic. We needed the silly sat-nav, the map and nerves of steel, but we did it – hurrah! We came out the other side unscathed, and not lost, which was a result.

For the first night in France, we had picked a site near to Fontainebleau, south of Paris, and an area we knew. In fact, we camped nearby over 30 years before when we were fresh-faced and courting. Our campsite, which is near Melun, is called the Belle Étoile – just a three-star site, but perfect for what we needed. We chose a pitch and I immediately got changed into my swimming costume. I'd set the intention to swim each day, so off I trotted and had the pool to myself. Refreshed and back at the van, I chilled out for a bit, mostly to sit and dry off with a glass of wine.

On the menu tonight was French onion soup. It's a favourite of mine, but I picked it for today, as historically it was invented in this area. The kings of France used to hunt in the forests and would enjoy a steaming bowl of soup afterwards at local hostelries. I know folks might think it's a bit peculiar making soup on holiday, but it is dead simple and makes a nice change from a heavy meal. We had it with bread and cheese on the side. John had a walk along the river that we can see from our pitch. He reported back that there were barges and houseboats, and took photos to show me, and it looked great.

I was thinking about my Grandpa a bit today, random I know, but we drove through the Somme area and of course it is forever remembered for the awful casualties and horrors of the Battle of the Somme in World War I. My Grandpa was a

veteran of the Somme, but he did at least return. All the same, he was part of it all, although he never said a word about it. I have his medals on the wall at home.

I am getting geared up for another move tomorrow. We are revisiting the site in Burgundy where we lived and worked for a full camping season back in 2009. It is about a three-hour drive from here, but I think it will be OK, compared to the tiring journey today anyway. We are staying two nights, so more time to relax and take everything in. I've already made a shopping list for tomorrow.

I've already discovered that motorhome-living is grand, but you do need to be prepared to avoid having to weigh anchor and go out to shops every day. I love shopping in French supermarkets, and it's a highlight of being here for me. I am going to buy everything I need for a few days and store it in our huge fridge.

Overall, day two was a good one. We're in France, I was less irritated by John than normal, and I had a lovely swim, so things are feeling good. I think I am going to turn in now. Tomorrow we can sleep in with no alarm to wake us, which will be a treat! The drop-down bed is very comfy, so with nothing to rush out for in the morning, hopefully I can catch some of the winks I have been missing.

– Day 2 Recipe –
FRENCH ONION SOUP

For centuries this classic soup was considered peasants' fare, but since the 18th century it has risen to very lofty heights. There are two theories about how it became so popular. One is that King Louis XV came home from hunting and there was only an onion, some butter, and some champagne in the kitchen – unlikely really, if you were a king – but anyway, the story goes that this delicious soup was developed for his palate at that point. The other theory is that the Duke of Lorraine tasted it in an inn in the Champagne area and loved it. He went on to popularise the recipe at the grand Palace of Versailles.

I made my campsite-friendly version in about 20 minutes. The key is to spend the first 10 minutes just gently softening the onions in butter, so they yield their natural sweetness. The soup can be vegetarian if you use vegetable stock. If you omit the butter and use more oil, it can be made vegan, which might not be authentic, but it will be tasty all the same.

Method
Melt the butter and oil in a large pan on a gentle heat. Add all the onions and mix. Cook very gently for about 10 minutes until the onions are very soft and sticky, stirring all the time.

Add the garlic, sugar and mustard and stir in the flour.

Add the wine and bring to a simmer. Lower the heat a bit and add the beef stock. Season to taste and then cook for about 10 more minutes until the soup has reduced by about half.

Serve with a round of toasted bread with melted cheese on the top, or if not practical, just some crusty French bread.

Ingredients (serves 2)
- Large knob of butter and a splash of olive oil
- 4 onions, finely sliced into rings
- 3 garlic cloves, crushed
- 1 teaspoon sugar
- 1 teaspoon Dijon mustard
- 1 tablespoon plain flour
- 200ml white wine
- 1 litre of beef stock (*see note above*)
- Salt and pepper

Soup is cuisine's kindest cousin.

Virginia Woolf

– *Day 3* –

GIGNY-SUR-SAÔNE,
SAÔNE-ET-LOIRE

Well **Diary, what can I say?** How do I explain how today has been... a total joy! Everything about it has been spot on. We were up at about six o'clock this morning, which is crackers, as that would make it 5:00am in the UK. We were raring to go, but we decided to chill out a bit and let the rush-hour traffic abate, plus I had ordered bread, and the campsite shop didn't open until 8:30. French bread is one of the simple pleasures in life – a baguette, or a pain, or a boule, or a flute or, as we called them as kids, a French stick! This campsite had the flutes in a big paper sack, and right next to them was a table with trays of croissants. The guy in the shop obviously wasn't expecting me to ask if I could take photos of his bread sack so early in the morning!

We packed up the motorhome and secured all areas – we learned quickly to check drawers and cupboards before moving off after our first drive, when the contents of the bathroom cabinet had come tumbling out. Our route today took us from the edge of Fontainebleau to Gigny-sur-Saône in Burgundy. A straightforward journey on the A6, a very quiet road and no wacky races involved today, thank the Lord. Beautiful weather, at least it was once the early morning mist had lifted, with everything bathed in sunshine.

We topped up with fuel in a service area and discovered that there are motorhome service points where you can top up water and empty the water tank. I was very impressed with that. We travelled on a bit longer and then pulled in at an 'aire'. These are small service areas with basic facilities like toilets, etc, but there are picnic benches, and sometimes a small playground, but they are always shady and very restful. I love

shopping. Anyway, we got in there with our chariot (the French name for a shopping trolley) and I was in my element. I had a good browse, and bought enough to last us at least four days. The helpful thing about writing this book is that because I've had to plan ahead, I know exactly what I'm cooking each day, so that makes shopping much easier. So that is a top tip – plan your menus and make a shopping list!

these spaces, because you can invariably see French people at their best, eating! Meals are taken seriously and are always an occasion. I have never seen a French family sitting in their car at a service area scoffing sandwiches out of triangular packets. No, out comes a tablecloth, and a cool bag with meats, cheese, fruit, salad and always a baguette. A lesson that I keep trying to learn.

Anyway, we ate our bread and cheese, and suitably refreshed we continued on our way. The landscape started to change a bit; it became more undulating, certainly prettier, as up until then it had been fields of wheat, but I suppose with all these French sticks to make that's an important crop! In no particular order on today's journey I have seen: a fox sitting in a field; a kestrel hovering over some prey; loads of poppies; hundreds of windmills; castles with turrets; lots of lavender; and finally, at Beaune, some vineyards. The journey was just over three hours long, but it didn't feel like three hours to me because I was so excited today. We are revisiting the site where we worked for a season back in 2009. We lived in a massive tent and had a brilliant time, although it was very full-on work. We were always at full speed, going like the clappers to keep up with the demands on us, but we always managed, and we loved the experience. When we finally turned off the motorway today, I was in familiar territory.

I wanted to call in at the supermarket to get some fresh supplies before setting up at the campsite. I know it is not just me that loves a French supermarket – I have had long conversations with like-minded friends about the joys of

We arrived at the campsite – Château de l'Epervière – and everything looked just the same, which I was pleased about. We were allocated a pitch, and we were set up in no time. It was too hot to put the kettle on, so we each had a small beer. I was as keen as mustard to have my daily swim and, as it was time for the bar to open for the afternoon, I suggested a trip to the pool and another beer. The pool was great, with a few other swimmers this time, unlike yesterday when I had the place to myself. We sipped our beers in the sunshine and headed off back to the motorhome.

We were situated next to one of two lakes. The fish were plopping at regular intervals, ducks were floating around, and I spotted some coypus (semi-aquatic mammals about the size of a guinea pig). I remember them from all those years ago, and was thrilled to see them thriving.

On to the Meal on the Move for today. When in Burgundy it's only right to cook with wine. Today it was coq au vin. I served it with green beans and some more crusty French bread. It was so delicious, with half a bottle of Burgundy in the pot and half a bottle to drink – perfect! I sat out until it was dropping dark, happy to watch the not-so-still waters – those coypus were making ripples as they swam about, a wonderful end to a fantastic day.

PS: I just checked our Premium Bonds, and we both had a little win. Winner, winner, chicken dinner!

– Day 3 Recipe –
COQ AU VIN

Another of my favourite dishes hails from Burgundy: coq au vin. Rich and luxurious, it is a proper dinner-party dish, but equally it deserves a place on your campsite menu – similar to a bourguignon, in that we start the sauce with onions, garlic, carrots and mushrooms. Of course, a quantity of red wine and sometimes a splash of brandy, and finished with some lovely shallots. Here is my take on it.

Ingredients (serves 2)

- 2 tablespoons olive oil
- 1 onion, chopped
- 4 rashers of chopped, smoked bacon or lardons
- 1 carrot, diced
- Punnet of mushrooms, halved
- 4 garlic cloves, crushed
- 2 tablespoons dried thyme
- 4 chicken thighs (*I used skinless/boneless, but on-the-bone is fine*)
- 1 tablespoon tomato purée
- 1 tablespoon plain flour
- Half a bottle of red wine
- Handful of shallots
- Salt and pepper
- Knob of butter
- Parsley to garnish

Method

Heat the oil in a large, lidded frying pan. Sweat the onion on a medium heat until soft and translucent.

Add the bacon/lardons, carrot, mushrooms, garlic and thyme. Sizzle for a couple of minutes.

Add the chicken, and cook for a few minutes until it is slightly browned. I sometimes cook on the gas BBQ for a few minutes instead, to start the cooking and to get some colour on the meat, before adding it to the pan.

Sprinkle over the flour and add the tomato purée, stir well and then pour in the wine. Place the lid on the pan and bring to the boil. Reduce to a simmer for 10 minutes, and then remove the lid and add the shallots. Reduce the heat further, and simmer and bubble for about 20 minutes until the sauce has reduced and the chicken is tender.

Season well with salt and pepper, add the butter for extra gloss, and serve with chopped parsley sprinkled on the top.

Serve with mashed potatoes or crusty bread, and a side of green beans.

I cook with wine,
sometimes I even put
it in the food.

WC Fields

– Day 4 –
GIGNY-SUR-SAÔNE,
SAÔNE-ET-LOIRE

Well, **Diary my friend,** what can I say about today? It was ace, fantastic, I enjoyed every second of it. We didn't do anything much, we stayed on site just mooching. Of course, we know the area well after having lived on this site for months all those years ago, so we don't feel we are missing out. First-up was, as usual, to go and collect today's daily bread. No bread sack at this campsite – a bit more elegant, with all the bread and pastries lined up on the shelves behind the till. There was a queue of campers out of the door, eager-beavers all wanting to get their morning fix of French stick. After that errand was done, we tucked into breakfast sitting outside on our lakeside pitch. Still waters first thing, not running deep though, as we discovered later today when a heron dropped by to say hello and it was standing ankle deep (do herons have ankles?) in the water.

I had a mission to accomplish this morning, to do with this book. I needed to get a good photograph for the front cover. A few things to consider when finding the perfect shot: it should have a good background, ideally a blue sky; a

grassy foreground; and yours truly plonked in front of the motorhome, at a table with some food preparation going on. This was a responsibility that I never would have thought might be resting on my shoulders. Our pitch, although perfectly located under trees and next to the lake, does not have the all-important grass. Seasoned campers will know there are two types of pitch: grass or hard-standing. My preference is always grass, however on some sites, like here, the pitches are allocated by the site management, and we were given a hard-standing. I knew there was no option to move, as the site is full, but I had a secret weapon. I know the guy in charge, and asked if he could suggest a good place to move the motorhome for a great photo location. He immediately suggested right in front of the château. He told me to wait until about 11:00am, when the sun would be in the perfect position to illuminate everything.

Anyway, Diary, I will cut to the chase. We moved the motorhome and started to get set up. It was quite funny how much interest these shenanigans created. First, we had two guys come up to explain that we couldn't pitch there. I told them we were not pitching, just having a few pics taken. Next, when the tripod came out, it was the ladies that approached, speaking in English, but with lovely Dutch and German accents. They were keen to praise the set-up and were asking if it was for Instagram. I told them it was for a book; they don't know me from Eve, but they seemed very

delighted about it all. I did get a bit snotty with John. I find it all quite stressful looking for the perfect photo every few hours, because I am only just learning this caper, but I am determined to succeed. I apologised to him, and he always takes it as par for the course and we go forward. I think we got some great photos; fingers are crossed!

I made tonight's dinner early, as I had some time on my hands, and it was set to be scorching later. I made mushroom bourguignon, and then sat down to watch the water. Our section of lake started to get some heavy-duty traffic by midday. The fish that I had heard plopping and splashing around yesterday were out in force and we could see them – loads of them, their dorsal fins sleekly cutting through the water's surface. I think some of them were carp, huge things. Fish creep me out quite a bit – I couldn't touch one unless it was on my plate in batter with lots of salt and vinegar, a side of chips and a slice of white bread and butter! For all of that, I was fascinated, especially when they started jumping. I wonder why they do that?

Later, we heard a nightingale, which was the best bit of the nature watch today. I heard a very unusual, well to my ears anyway, birdsong, so John and I tried to figure out where it was perched but we couldn't see it. I downloaded an app that can identify birdsong, and lo and behold it was a common nightingale. Not the one Anne Shelton sang about in Berkeley Square, although that must have been a posh nightingale. Diary, I am showing my age now when I can recall the name of a popular post-war singer! Next, the heron came and then an egret. The egret was very quick and bagged the most lunch from what I could see. The heron went for bigger prey, and gobbled up a very resistant frog – yuk, yuk, yuk!

I went for my swim, so one hundred per cent success so far with that intention. John sat in the bar with a beer, and I joined him for a rosé wine, well two in fact as they were only small glasses. We got chatting to a young woman from New Zealand who was on a four-month tour with her Yorkshireman husband and four kids – three boys and a baby girl. They were all enjoying the motorhome dream, a big motorhome too – I spotted it with lots of washing and kids' toys outside. She took our photographs together, and I really enjoyed meeting her.

It was easy to warm up the bourguignon for tea, and I served it with some pasta, which heralded a 'yuk, yuk' from John on the pasta – he has never been a fan. We had plenty of bread, and finished off our dinner with a lovely raspberry tartlet that I bought from the supermarket. The patisserie is always top-end wherever you buy it in France. The ducks came up to beg for crumbs, and then the heron was back, pacing about like Uriah Heep. Finally, a very late appearance from the coypus, just as dusk was falling. I found a notice by the lake further up the site, warning us not to feed them, as they can be unpredictable and quite cross little creatures, belying their cute little faces! Ah well, as is often the case, not just a pretty face!

Night, night, Diary, I am bushed. It has been a great day... onwards to our next destination tomorrow.

− Day 4 Recipe −
MUSHROOM BOURGUIGNON

Beef bourguignon is my signature dish! I developed my version after living on a campsite in Burgundy for six months and sampling the 'real thing' in the campsite restaurant many times. A beef version takes many hours to simmer and become tender and delicious, so I have created this mushroom version, which also happens to be accidentally vegan!

If you can only get large shallots, you will need to modify the recipe, either splitting them or using less, as if they are large, they take longer to cook. I have been known to just halve or quarter an onion if I can't get shallots at all. For the stock I use a cube or the new style stockpots with water! Leftovers make a tasty 'œufs en meurette' for breakfast (see inset photo)!

Ingredients (serves 2)

- 2 tablespoons oil (*I used garlic infused*)
- 1 onion, finely chopped
- 1 carrot, chopped into small dice
- 4 handfuls of mixed variety mushrooms chopped chunkily (*at least 15*)
- 4 large garlic cloves, crushed
- 2 tablespoons tomato purée
- 2 tablespoons plain flour
- 1 tablespoon dried thyme
- 1 tablespoon Dijon mustard
- 8 (or more) small shallots (*ideally the size of a small pickled onion*)
- Half a bottle (*or more*) red wine (*Burgundy preferably*)
- 250ml vegetable stock
- Salt and pepper to taste
- Large handful chopped parsley to garnish

Method

Heat the oil in a large, lidded frying pan. Cook the onion on a gentle heat for about five minutes to allow the sweetness to develop and become caramelised slightly.

Add the carrots, garlic, mushrooms, purée, thyme, mustard and the shallots and cook for a few minutes to allow the mushrooms to release their juices and then sprinkle over the flour (which will thicken the sauce).

Continue to cook until the mushrooms have wilted a bit then add the wine and stock. Bring to the boil and then reduce to a simmer with the lid partially on.

When everything is starting to become very saucy, remove the lid and continue to cook gently to reduce the consistency to a glossy thick sauce. When the shallots and carrots are tender, season to taste with salt and pepper and scatter over the chopped parsley.

This goes well with pasta, rice mash or gratin potatoes, or of course a lovely crusty baguette!

Nature alone is antique and the oldest art the mushroom.

Thomas Carlyle

– Day 5 –
VALLON-PONT-D'ARC
ARDÈCHE

What a difference a day makes. We woke up to a very wet campsite this morning. I had heard the thunder rattling around during the night, so I wasn't really surprised to see how much rain there had been. The campsite is prone to flooding, as it is very close to the big river Saône. I remember when we worked at the site all those years ago being told of rowing boats used to check for stray tents after a flood. Thankfully, it wasn't anything like that this morning and already the sun was peeping out.

We moved on today, heading further south and towards the Ardèche Gorge. As we headed onto the motorway, the dark clouds started to lift and by the time we were near Lyon it was sunny again. We crossed the Rhône and were staggered at its width – massive! We had an uneventful journey except for one thing. We were trying to pay for our road toll at a pay booth, and of course, as with many things, they are no longer operated by a human. The ticket I was feeding into the machine was spat out at me time after time, with some French

words on the screen that I guessed meant that the computer said 'NO'. After trying a few more times, with the wretched barrier still preventing us from leaving, I pressed an assistance button. Mustering all my French, I managed to say 'Le ticket ne marche pas', which means 'The ticket does not work', and a lady came back, rabbiting in quick-fire French. Anyway, she worked some magic, we paid the bill and the barrier opened and allowed us to travel further. Oh, and a family pack of plain crisps fell on John's head from the shelves above as we drove along. That made us laugh, but taught us something too, as it could have been something heavy and we wouldn't have been laughing then!

On this journey I spotted signs saying Beaujolais and Côtes de Rhône, and soon enough we saw loads of vineyards on sloping hillsides. The mountains in the far distance were the Rhône Alps and I could tell we were getting further south when I started to see the tall, spindly needle shapes of the cypress

trees. There were lots of red kites circling around the by-now blue skies.

The signs started to tell us we were getting closer to our destination – near Montélimar – and I knew we were getting close. Famous for nougat, or as my mum always says 'nugget' (just like she says 'berret' for beret – her command of French is not even close to mine and mine is 'pas bon'). I like it when the architecture and the style of roof tile tells you where you are in the world. Red terracotta roof tiles speak south of France, and this is what we started to see on the last half hour of the journey today.

We came off the busy road and started heading up into 'them thar hills' and small villages, all quaint. We saw one restaurant in a tiny sleepy village, which was full of local folk dining al fresco in a cute courtyard. It's Sunday today, so Sunday lunch there was where it was at!

Eventually we got to our site. First impressions were that it was amazing, bathed in sunshine, blue skies, blue pool, right on the riverbank – so gorgeous. We rushed to the pitch, and got changed for a swim. I could hardly believe it when John got his trunks on, as he never ever takes a dip. He did today, and it was great to splash around together. However, dark clouds were looming, and a guy from the campsite started taking all the parasols down, then we heard thunder.

We scarpered out of the pool and headed for the bar next door. We ordered coffee, ice creams and a beer, and guess what happened next? We were rained in. The heavens opened and everywhere was dark. Undeterred, we ordered more drinks. Fortunately the weather improved quite quickly, otherwise we would have been very tiddly indeed! When we got back to the motorhome, we had a technical problem that resulted in a bit of a falling out between us, well a big one really. All my promises to be kinder were broken in one hit. Thankfully, a helpful German guy on the next pitch came over waving a 'superior' can of lubricating spray, and we managed to fix the issue.

It was then time for dinner, with peace now restored in base camp. Ardèche bombine was on the menu, which is a little-known local dish that was surprisingly delicious given that the main ingredients are potatoes and carrots, with a bit of bacon in the mix. At least no pasta tonight, so John was happier.

So Diary, like I said, it has been a mixed bag today, but that is life, this much I do know. We have plans tomorrow to take a canoe on the river, depending on the forecast, but I am hoping we manage it, as it is on my bucket list for this trip and we only have tomorrow before we buzz off again.

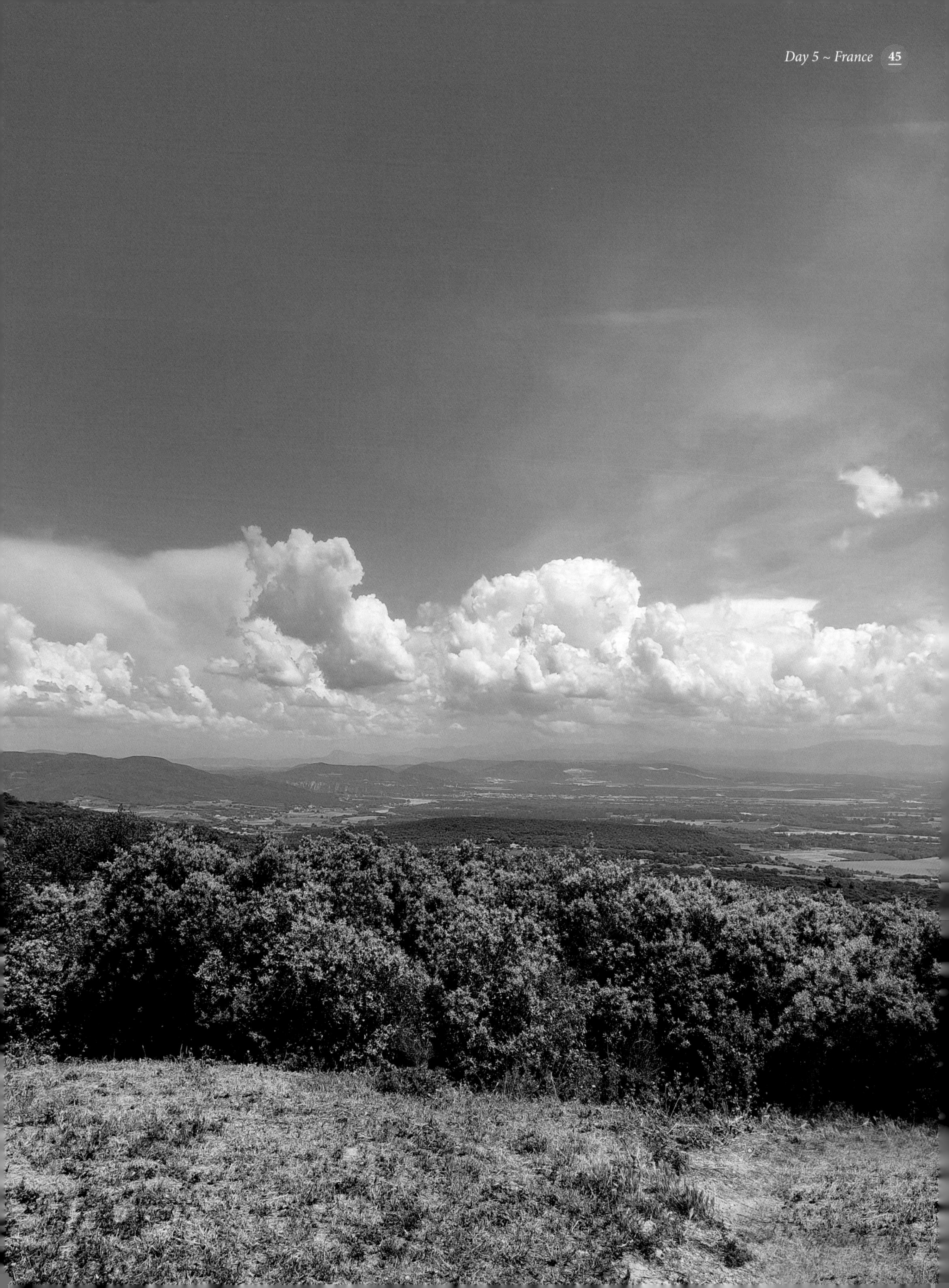

– Day 5 Recipe –
ARDÈCHE BOMBINE

I came across this dish whilst researching the Ardèche region of France. Fundamentally a peasant dish comprised mostly of potatoes, there were many variations of the bombine, but potatoes were always the key ingredient.

This dish could easily be vegetarian, or even vegan, as meat is not in every version. Add or remove things as you wish.

Ingredients (serves 2)

- 2 tablespoons olive oil
- 1 onion, finely chopped
- 1 pack lardons *(remove for vegan)*
- 2 large potatoes, finely diced *(I did not peel mine)*
- 2 carrots, finely diced
- 4 garlic cloves, crushed
- 1 tablespoon plain flour
- Salt and pepper
- 1 tablespoon thyme
- 1 large glass of red or white wine *(optional)*
- 1 tablespoon tomato purée
- 1 chicken stock cube/pot *(vegetable for vegetarian/vegan)*
- 1 tablespoon Worcestershire sauce *(omit or use Henderson's Relish for vegetarian/vegan)*
- Handful cherry tomatoes
- Handful black olives
- Water *(approx. 500ml)*
- Fresh parsley to garnish

Method

Heat the oil in a large, lidded frying pan. Gently fry the onion until soft and translucent. Add the lardons and cook for a minute or so to release some juices.

Add the potatoes and carrots and mix well. Sauté the mixture for about five minutes, stirring often.

Add the garlic, thyme, salt and pepper, then sprinkle over the flour and mix well.

Add all the other ingredients and a cupful of the water. Bring to a boil and then add the rest of the water bit by bit. Cook with the lid on, stirring often, until the vegetables are tender. Add more water as needed. The whole dish takes no more than 30 minutes to cook, and the objective is for the potatoes to absorb liquid until they are tender.

Remove the pan lid once almost all the liquid has been absorbed, and cook until the liquid has been fully absorbed.

Garnish with parsley.

If more of us valued food, cheer and song over hoarded gold, it would be a merrier world.

JRR Tolkien

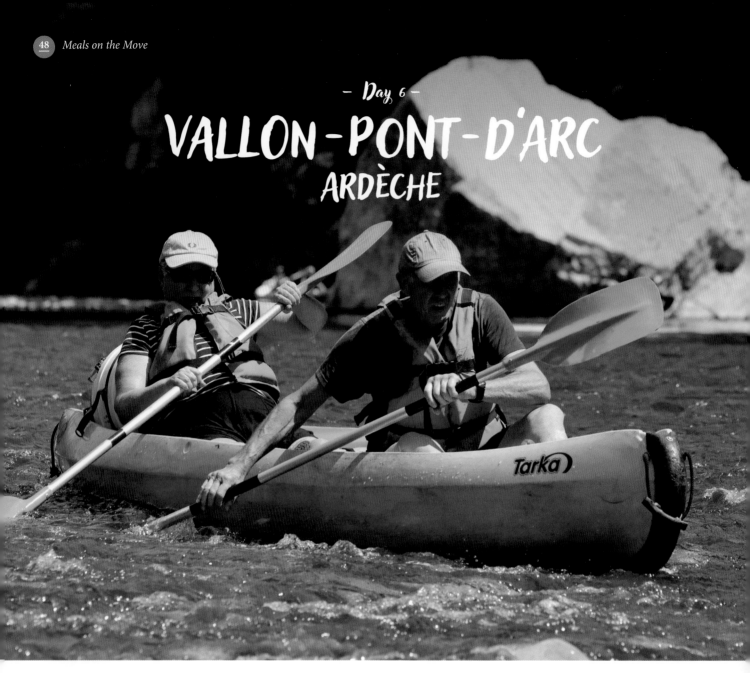

– *Day 6* –
VALLON-PONT-D'ARC
ARDÈCHE

Diary, today has been nigh-on perfect. After the frustrations of yesterday it is fantastic to be back on top of everything. When I woke up this morning, once again at daft o'clock, things felt better. The sun had got its hat on, and we had plans in place to do exciting things. You know how I set my intentions at the start of the holiday, well one thing I wanted to do was to make sure we try to actually do stuff on this trip. In the past I have either been too disorganised to put plans in place, or too tight with my budget to spend some cash on excursions, entrance fees or trips.

The exciting plan in question for today was to hire a canoe and take a trip down the Ardèche river. The campsite we are staying at has a canoe station about half a minute's stroll from our pitch, and it is right on the riverside, so there was no excuse not to bite the bullet. I sussed it all out yesterday: it was going to cost us 50 euros to hire the stuff, which I didn't think was too bad a price.

Anyway, the only dilemma to solve was how to ensure our belongings didn't go sailing down the river in the event of a capsize situation. We were given a big plastic barrel to strap securely to the canoe, but we were told they couldn't guarantee how watertight it was. Hum? What about getting photographs then? My phone is too precious to risk a plunge into the Ardèche, so I decided not to take it at all. John bought some zip-lock plastic sandwich bags from the shop and he put his cameras into those and then into the barrel. We packed some water and some sandwiches, then off we went.

As with many things in life, it was not as easy as it looked. There is no way to be elegant getting in a canoe, and if you want to keep dry, don't bother at all. My bum was soaked before I even had a paddle in my hand. Anyway, we eventually paddled off, I was at the back and meant to steer, John was at the front and he was the stroker. It took a few minutes to get synchronised – and that is not our strong point even in everyday life, let alone on a river, but we did start to pull together and move in the correct direction. The guy had told us a bit about where we might find tricky spots and how to deal with them, and if the worst happened and we went overboard, what to do. It all sounded straightforward, but in

The next problem came in the form of some rapids. Nothing much, just a bit wobbly I was thinking as we approached. Not so! Around and around we went in ever increasing circles, and then finally, 'splosh', we went over, capsized! My sandals went floating away, just like John's flip-flops, and my hat too.

reality it was hard. For a start, my arms were tired after only a couple of hundred yards, but then we discovered you could stop paddling and just drift a bit. All well and good, but before we knew where we were, we had drifted to the side and were beached on rocks in about six inches of water.

We tried and tried to free ourselves, but nothing worked. A few metres away were a couple of photographers on a tiny island and they were gesturing to us. I worked out they were saying to stand up. Fat chance of me doing that, but John had a go and toppled over. Off went his flip-flops and away they sailed with not a care in the world. With great difficulty and much cursing, John, flip-flopless, on the rocky riverbed, freed the canoe and managed to get back on board. We paddled for all we were worth to get away from the embarrassing situation. We paddled by the photographers and managed to grimace for the camera, and off we went downriver.

It was a bit hair-raising, very exhilarating and I could feel the adrenalin pumping. We scrabbled around and managed to hang on to our upturned canoe, then dragged it to the riverbank, and with the help of some lads who were watching from the shore, we got it on to dry land for a bit.

We took a breather and then got back on board. A family came sailing towards us holding up John's flip-flops and one of my sandals. They explained how they managed the rapids, which was to just lift the paddles and go with the flow (is that where that phrase originates from, I wonder?). Thus advised, we continued with more success, but not without some near misses. John was now discovering a few injuries from his tumble, and his elbows and knees were cut and bleeding a bit, but he soldiered on. Then, ahoy! Someone brought me my other lost sandal. Just like the Cinderella of the river, I now was re-shod, the world turned, and all was well once again.

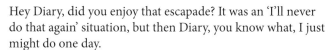

Hey Diary, did you enjoy that escapade? It was an 'I'll never do that again' situation, but then Diary, you know what, I just might do one day.

When we were waiting for the bus to take our soggy, sunburned and, in John's case, battered bodies back to the campsite, we saw vultures soaring way above us. I have seen these huge birds of prey before in a region not far from here as the bird flies, or in this case the vulture flies, in the Cevennes. I recognised them and it was quite thrilling. This trip has been a bit of a wildlife tour, and we are getting to see all sorts of things.

That dip in the river counted as my swim of the day, so no trip to the pool aujourd'hui. After a hot shower and a change into dry clothes I was back outside our motorhome basking in the sun. John went for his shower, and in seconds the weather changed and another enormous thunderstorm hit us, along with hailstones. Yesterday stranded in the bar was good, but today John was stranded in the gents' sanitation block. Oh well, the joys of camping life once more.

The sun was out after about half an hour, and John sauntered back, with much moaning about his injuries, which were starting to become very visible, with bumps and bruises and so on. I told him the blessing of the situation was that at least he wasn't cracked on the head, and his response to that was it might have knocked some sense into him! He is not a bad old stick as sticks go!

I made dinner in the glorious evening sunshine. Tonight, it was ratatouille. We're not quite in the correct region for it, but we are moving to Provence tomorrow, so it's a flavour of things to come. John is not keen on Mediterranean vegetables (he is more of a peas and carrots man), so I tempted his tastebuds with a bit of BBQ sausage – it did the trick, and clean plates all round.

Well Diary, I feel we have had a very good day. I am sure we will get plenty of good-quality winks tonight.

Bonne nuit!

– Day 6 Recipe –
RATATOUILLE

Ratatouille makes the most of the glorious Mediterranean vegetables. It is a very versatile dish. It can be a main meal, served as a side dish, or as a toast topper! It is of course vegan too. The fennel and Pernod are typical of the area, but not essential if you have neither in the cupboard!

Ingredients (serves 2)

- 2 tablespoons olive oil
- 1 aubergine, cubed
- 1 tablespoon salt
- 1 courgette, sliced
- 1 red pepper, sliced
- 1 onion, chopped
- 4 garlic cloves, crushed
- 1 tablespoon tomato ketchup
- 1 tablespoon tomato purée
- 400g can chopped tomatoes
- 150ml white wine
- 1 tablespoon oregano
- 1 teaspoon fennel seeds *(optional)*
- 1 tablespoon Pernod *(optional)*
- Salt and pepper
- Fresh basil to garnish

Method

Heat the oil in a large frying pan and sauté the aubergine until it has softened a little and is taking on some colour.

If the aubergine has guzzled all the oil, add a splash more, then add the courgette and cook for a few minutes. Next, add the onion, pepper, and the garlic.

Keep stirring regularly, and when the vegetables have softened a little, add the oregano, fennel seeds, ketchup, tomato purée and chopped tomatoes.

Add the wine and bring to a boil, then reduce to a simmer, and season with salt and pepper to taste. Continue to cook until the liquid has almost gone.

Take off the heat and pour in the Pernod, if using. Scatter with fresh, torn basil leaves and serve as a side dish, or with rice or pasta as a main course. Any leftovers can be reheated the next day, and served on toasted bread for lunch, or even with poached eggs!

If you are what you eat, then I only want to be the good stuff!

Remy Ratatouille

– Day 7 –
VOLONNE,
ALPES-DE-HAUTE-PROVENCE

Diary, I can't believe we have been seven whole days on this journey together, it is flying by. So far it has been absolutely wonderful, with only one slight glitch in seven days, so not bad and that was a technical issue that our German neighbour helped us sort. I reckon that is quite a result, as John and I are not an ideal match in many ways. I correct that slightly, we are matched in some ways, and complement each other, but in some areas, well, enough said!

Today has been almost 100 percent fabulous. We got up this morning and left the campsite in the Ardèche. The first thing on the to-do list was to go to the supermarket and stock up with ingredients, beer and wine, plus fill the tank with fuel. I have already found a bit of a routine around the motorhome, and setting off to a new destination feels better if we have done all the housekeeping before we go. We then have no anxieties about running low on diesel, or having to find somewhere to buy fresh milk, for example. Diary, just for the record, fresh milk is not that common in France, and I don't like UHT on my cornflakes.

We had consulted with Sally the sat-nav (we've given her a name now!) and the road map to decide which route we

should take to Provence. There were two choices: one slow but cheaper, and the other fast and expensive. Sometimes, fast and expensive is the way to go, if the wish is to get through some duller areas and get to the destination ASAP. Today was not one of those days. Tired already of autoroutes and paying the hefty tolls, we decided to take the Route Touristique or, as we say in the UK, the scenic route. Sally was telling us there was only 20 minutes' difference in time anyway, but she was wrong! A three-hour journey turned into a five-hour journey. Not complaining though, it was wonderful! Let me tell you about it.

The route took us cross-country from the Drôme department through to the Alpes Côte d'Azur. Up in the mountains, the huge Mont Ventoux, often referred to as the Giant of Provence, could be seen from afar. John was very excited about this. The mountain is one of the most famous in Europe, and is often featured in the Tour de France – it is one of the great climbs of the cycling world. Tom Simpson, one of cycling's heroes back in the sixties, sadly died on Ventoux whilst competing. Anyway, our journey took us closer and closer to the Giant and we managed to stop in a layby to take in the views. The weather was perfect today too, bright skies and warm, but not so hot that it boiled your brain being outside. Two things that I saw a lot of today as we travelled along, were bright yellow broom and vineyards, with people amongst the vines tending them. I wondered if the vineyard workers kept a note of where they had got up to when they finished for the day, because those rows of vines are huge! We

moved first through rolling hills, before climbing up towards the mountains. It was edge-of-the-seat stuff for me: I really have a problem with heights, and I find it very nerve-wracking when you are driving along a small road where two vehicles can barely just pass each other, with a sheer drop on your side of the road and only a matter of inches from going over and it being curtains. Much of the time I was peeping through my almost-shut eyes (I wasn't the driver!), and I was very pleased when those sections of the journey were over and we were on the downward spiral of hairpin bends, back to the security of flatter terrain.

We drove through several small villages and towns, waving as we went. Old men with broken teeth grinned back, and young men with glasses of wine and cigarettes were too busy in their conversations to notice us. We saw towering castles and ice-blue streams. We drove under a canopy of huge plane trees and finally, so many hours after leaving the Ardèche, we arrived at our next port of call, Volonne, a small town in Provence.

At the campsite we had a frustrating first hour. We were booked onto a large pitch with water and electricity, called a Grande Comfort. It was a take-your-pick of the

'emplacements' right next to the river. Sounded idyllic, but not so! The pitches were large, but being near the river, the ones available were a bit boggy, and worse, had lots of mosquitoes! Also, there were mobile homes being installed right behind, and JCBs were digging out the ground all around the area.

We decided to ask for an inferior emplacement. This was agreed, and we found a smashing spot which also had water and electricity, but no diggers and no biters. We also have two olive trees on our pitch!

We settled in quickly and I made for the pool. It was warm water, gorgeous, and only me in it initially, until a child came and jumped in right in my face – always happens, eh? I can tell John is getting a bit cheesed off having to take all the photographs, but I have been explaining how important it is that I get some decent pictures. It is, Diary – where would you and I be without evidence?

Anyway, John went off to take some pictures for himself. He is more mountains and birds than wives and swimming pools in the photo-taking department, I understand that, and encouraged him to have a wander off while I prepared our meal.

Yes, at the end of the day it is all about the food in my world. I made a lovely Niçoise salad. Now once again, John is not really a salad man, but he did scoff his plateful, as it had new potatoes and boiled eggs, both two of his preferred foods. The main issue he had with this salad was the olives, which are now added to the list (that just keeps growing!) of things that John won't eat! He also considers tuna 'poor man's salmon' as, when he was a child in the fifties, tinned salmon was considered upmarket and a real treat. Despite his grumbles, both our plates were cleared and I thought it was delicious.

Anyway Diary, it's time to bed down for the night. It has been a wonderful day all things considered; I have a lot to give thanks for today, it's just the best.

– *Day 7 Recipe* –
SALAD NIÇOISE

Originating in Nice, which is a glorious, glamorous city on the French Riviera, this salad conjures up the sunshine just by looking at it. It is so easy to put together, and heaped on a platter and enjoyed with a cold glass of wine, it is very dreamy indeed!

Ingredients (serves 2)

- 1 crispy lettuce, shredded
- 1 large tomato, cut into chunks
- A handful of cooked French green beans
- 2 hard-boiled eggs, halved
- A handful of small new potatoes, cooked and cooled
- Half a red onion, peeled and sliced into rings
- 1 can of tuna, drained
- A handful of black olives
- A few anchovies *(or a splash of Worcestershire sauce)*
- Salt and pepper
- 4 tablespoons white wine vinegar
- 1 tablespoon extra-virgin olive oil
- Fresh dill or parsley to garnish

Method

Whisk together the oil and the vinegar (and Worcestershire sauce if using) to make a dressing.

Assemble all the other ingredients on a large platter and then pour the dressing over. Garnish with dill or parsley.

*Man cannot live
by bread alone.
Every once in a while
he needs a salad.*

Woody Allen

– Day 8 –
VOLONNE,
ALPES-DE-HAUTE-PROVENCE

A lovely calm and relaxing last day in France, at least for this leg of the tour. The sun was up and about good and early, and after breakfast we walked into Volonne. I chose the campsites, wherever possible, to be able to visit something either on foot, bus or train, because taking the motorhome out every day would be a slight pest. Volonne, a small, very old town, is only a kilometre from this site. The town is built on a hillside and there are small alleyways running up and down and from side to side via ancient stone steps, all of them with houses on either side as you walk along – some very tall houses, and some of them very small, with the tiniest of entrance doors. There were patches of gardens and allotments dotted around too, and quite a few cats, fierce and suspicious-looking as they hurried on by.

Eventually, and only by chance, we found the main square. There was the usual café in the centre and a restaurant with the week's menus on a blackboard hanging from a chain. We wandered down the main street which, as is typical, had the plane trees looking magnificent and shady. We sat outside the Mairie (town hall) complete, as usual, with the Tricolore flapping in the breeze. Outside was the pétanque pitch, but it

was deserted this morning, as it tends to be a game enjoyed in the afternoon or evening. We had a very good café crème sitting in the sunshine with the locals. We called for a few provisions at a tiny shop and set off back to the campsite. Inevitably we got lost, those little alleyways befuddled us, but Sally sat-nav once more came to our aid and we eventually retraced our steps and got home just in time for lunch.

Here at Volonne we are on the 'Route Napoléon', the famous route that Napoleon Bonaparte took in 1815 with his army when he escaped from exile in Elba. It took him from Antibes in the south to Grenoble, and he went right through Volonne – there was a painting on the wall depicting it by the ancient 'lavarie' (launderette) in the town.

I did a week's worth of washing and got it pegged out to dry in the afternoon sun, and then I prepared this evening's recipe. One of my favourites, although it's a bit of a cliché, Chicken Provençal – chicken cooked in a bright tomato sauce with the tiniest hint of spice. I cooked it outside on my stove and it was so nice, cooking away in the midday sun (being the mad dog that I am) under the shade of an olive tree, perfection!

When the dish was cool enough it went into the fridge, and I went into the pool. Still 100 percent compliance with that intention. If I hadn't made that commitment to you Diary, and hence to myself, I would not be swimming every day – the effort, in the afternoon sun, may have proved too much for me!

The pool complex here is very good, and the setting is magnificent. As I floated about, I thanked my lucky stars (and the people that enabled this trip) for my good fortune. I keep trying to live in the moment, but I am just a human being and not a dog. Sometimes I forget to live in the moment and my mind starts whirring too fast! Dogs always look happy, come rain or shine, they trot along and for sure they are thinking of nothing but that second, that nanosecond of time and place.

I returned to the van to encourage John to come out and play. He did and we returned to the pool area to have a beer together. The site is very quiet; just now there was only a handful of other people in the bar with us, and a few splashing around in the pool. We returned to the motorhome accompanied by a dog. Perhaps my earlier musings were a lesson in 'be careful what you wish for'. I had conjured up our very own dog, a small black and tan version of something – not a regular breed. He was very obviously a male if you get my drift – and if you don't you would if you saw how many times he cocked his leg – and followed us happily back to the van, docked tail twitching a little wag. I just saved my potted herbs that were on the grass getting some sun from

the attentions of that cocked leg. John tried to shoo the dog away, but he was having none of it and settled down for a snooze. We went about our own business and ignored him, and eventually he took the hint and padded off somewhere else.

Diary, I am still trying to figure out a cover shot for the book. My team back in the UK have been advising me and suggested that a basket of fruit and vegetables might look the part, on my arm, in front of the motorhome. Unable to locate a basket shop in the town this morning I suddenly hit upon an idea, a flash of inspiration. There might be something in the skip on site? Maybe a crate, one of the things that are filled with produce at the market. The inspiration was divine and, as if by magic, exactly the thing was sitting on top of the cardboard packaging in the recycling bin. Hurrah! I have my prop if baskets continue to elude me.

Back now to dinner. Tonight, the meal has nothing to disappoint John, apart from the olives and sundried tomatoes, but he can pick those out easily enough. I set the table under the olive tree, and it was picture perfect until… NO! More dark clouds and rumbles of thunder. Down came the rain once again. Table abandoned, we reset ourselves and ate our dinner in the motorhome, which of course is very comfortable. It was delicious, a success in every way.

Onwards tomorrow to pastures new. Sanremo in Italy. I'm a bit dubious, as I have very little experience of Italy and none of Italians. The reputation of hot-blooded lovers is not one I am likely to be testing out, but their reputation as mad drivers may well be. Bit nervous, but excited at the same time.

Bed calls, night night!

– Day 8 Recipe –

PROVENÇAL CHICKEN

This is the ever-popular chicken casserole of the area. It is rich and red in colour, another plate of sunshine!

Ingredients (serves 2)

- 2 tablespoons olive oil
- 4 boneless and skinless chicken thighs *(or breasts if available, if not bone and skin on is fine)*
- 1 onion, sliced
- 1 red pepper, sliced
- 4 garlic cloves, crushed
- 1 tablespoon oregano
- 1 tablespoon Worcestershire sauce *(or tinned anchovies)*
- 1 tablespoon plain flour
- 150ml rosé or white wine
- 500g carton passata or chopped tomatoes
- 200ml chicken stock
- Half a jar sundried tomatoes
- 1 tablespoon ketchup
- Handful black olives
- Salt and pepper
- Torn fresh basil to garnish

Method

Heat the oil in a large frying pan and brown the chicken on all sides, which should take about five minutes. Remove to a plate.

Soften the onions in the pan on a low heat for about five minutes and then add the red peppers and cook for a couple of minutes. Add the garlic, the herbs, and the Worcestershire sauce. Scatter the flour over and mix well. Add the wine, ketchup and chicken stock, and bring to a boil for a few minutes.

Return the chicken to the pan and reduce to a simmer. Cook until the liquid has reduced, and the sauce is quite thick. This takes about 20 minutes.

Add the sundried tomatoes and the olives, and season well with salt and pepper. Scatter the basil leaves on top just before serving.

Serve with rice or pasta.

One cannot think well, love well or sleep well if one has not dined well.

Virginia Woolf

Romeo, Romeo, wherefore art thou Romeo?

Italy is a land of romance, a land of passion, a land of hot, worldly men, a land of strong, beautiful women, of sopranos, of tenors, of old-fashioned nonnas minding brown-eyed bambinos, of Roman emperors and white-robed popes, of gladiators, of soaring cathedrals and of Renaissance artists.

Italy is shaped like a high-heeled boot, a sexy boot at that – a shape that hints at passion. It is noisy and fast-paced in some places and quiet, serene and magical in others.

It also has great pizza and don't get me started on the pasta!

I have visited Italy three times so far. The first was for John's 60th birthday. I booked flights to Milan as a surprise, and I booked a caravan on the banks of Lake Garda for our accommodation. Our second visit was during the time we were working for the holiday company, based in the Côte d'Azur, when our two daughters were also working for the same company and they were living in Italy on the Adriatic coast, close to Venice. Katharine was the area manager and Vanessa was a high-season rep. When it was Vanessa's birthday, we took a long weekend and drove along the Italian Riviera and down to the Adriatic to visit them. The third occasion was a coach trip to the Dolomites in the very north of the country in 2022. So really, I have only dipped into the country and I'm very keen to see more.

I feel connected to Italy, despite my limited visits. My dad spent the whole of the Second World War fighting in the Italian campaign. He did most of the scrapping way down in the south, in Sicily and Monte Cassino. My dad fancied himself as a linguist, and would often speak in Italian to me – of course he could have been speaking nonsense, but I thought it sounded great. He always referred to tomatoes as pomodori even when he was a very old man. I don't think he had much opportunity to sample Italian food – though, it was wartime and I guess things were grim everywhere.

My dad's experiences in Italy did not filter into our kitchen in Featherstone as I grew up. My only taste of any sort of pasta was spaghetti, which I didn't know was pasta because it came in a tin and I had it on toast as an alternative to baked beans! I can clearly remember the first time I tried to make 'spag bol'. I was 19, so it would be in 1977, my friend Susan from the bank

turned up at my house with a pack of spaghetti that she had spotted in the supermarket. It was in a royal blue packet and was about as long as my outstretched arm. We put together a concoction including minced beef, stock cubes and grated carrot and set about trying to cook these long strands of brittle pasta in a big pan of boiling water. Suffice to say I have come a along way pasta-wise since then!

To get into Italy on this trip I particularly wanted to retrace the route the way we had on the visit to my daughters. We travelled along the coastal road in France past Nice and Monaco and then entered Italy and drove all the way along the Italian Riviera. The blue sky and blue sea were a sight to behold, and I remember feeling very free, very warm and full of energy and of course excited.

I'm also looking forward to eating well in Italy. What do we think of then when we consider Italian food, pizza, pasta and...? Like everywhere there are regional differences often depending on the climate and what can be successfully grown. When I was in the Dolomites, I noticed acres and acres of apple orchards, so I wasn't surprised to see apple cake served everywhere. At Lake Garda there was fish on every menu, recipes evolve from what people can find locally to where they are living. In the north of the country, you are more likely to be offered pasta with a cream sauce whereas further south it would be light olive oil or tomato-based ragù.

Pizza originated from Naples many centuries ago but is now of course probably one of the most popular foods in the world. The story goes that in 1889 Queen Margherita was visiting Naples and new toppings were created for her to choose from. Her choice was simple: cheese, tomato and basil – the colours of the Italian flag, hence it was named the Margherita. Controversy is attached to pizzas though – should it be deep pan or thin and crispy? Does pineapple belong on a pizza? Perhaps on this trip I will get some answers!

I understand that the Italian temperament is very different to the French. I rather like the cool, almost detached attitude that can prevail in France. It will be interesting to meet some Italians and get up close to those hot-blooded types. Is it something to do with the weather I wonder, where this reputation comes from? I don't think it is the Latin in them, I studied Latin at school, and there was a lack of passion dripping from the pages of my exercise books, that I do know.

Of course, I am not visiting the whole of Italy on this trip. I am only getting down as far as Tuscany, so I am dipping my toe into the food and the culture, and I am looking forward to new experiences and look forward to learning more about the tastes and textures of Italy.

Buon viaggio!

– Day 9 –

SANREMO, LIGURIA

Dear Diary, what a day we have had: the good, the bad and the ugly! Well, that's a bit of an exaggeration. It's been very good. A little bit snaggy in parts and not ugly in the slightest. We made it to Italy. Now I am a bit out of my comfort zone here; I know France very well, but I haven't got a clue about Italy. I am excited to be somewhere different!

To kick the day off, we packed up the motorhome and headed once again to a supermarket to fill the tank and the fridge. That done, we set the sat-nav, our friend Sally, to take us via the high road to Italy. We decided once more to take the tourist and cheaper road. Funny how we didn't go that way… Before we knew what was happening, we were on the autoroute heading to Nice. I must have pressed OK when Sally told me there was a faster route, but hey ho, onwards, it was fast, and it was fun.

When we got right down towards the Côte d'Azur, I started to recognise places and signs from when we lived on a campsite there in 2010. However, I would have recognised it from the landscape alone and the light. I think Van Gogh really liked the light in that part of France, but don't quote me on it. The conifers are short and stubby, a bit mushroom-shaped, and the earth is red and dusty. I know that is not a very flattering description, but believe me it's attractive in its own way.

Before we knew what was happening, we were driving along the coast, with the bright blue Mediterranean Sea away to our right. We drove through countless tunnels heading closer and closer to Italy. My phone was the first to tell me we had arrived – there was no big sign and no borders to check in at. We stopped at the first Italian toll booth and alas it would not dispense a ticket. It did allow us through though, so I just thought 'hurrah, a freebie'. We quickly arrived at Sanremo, our destination for today, but we couldn't get in! The toll booth at this end required a ticket. I pressed a big red knob (pardon the expression) and had my first altercation with an Italian man. His booming voice was telling me to put a ticket in the slot, so using my non-existent Italian I replied: 'No ticket, no ticket'; he answered me in English asking, 'Where did you come from?' I say 'France', he says 'France?' I quickly registered that France is a big place and he might charge

me a fortune, so I respond 'Menton' (a town close to the border). On the digital screen up comes the price, 5.70 euros – not bad! – I paid and we got through the barrier.

Now in Sanremo, the sat-nav was guiding us to the campsite, allegedly. I say that because once again we went wrong and found ourselves at a dead end, parked up next to a few tatty campervans with folk camping wild. John thought this was our site. If I hadn't been so hot and bothered that would have been funny.

Anyway, we retraced our steps and to cut a long story short we found the site, like an oasis in the desert. Lush, fringed with palms and fronds of other greenery, jasmine-scented hedgerows and right by the sea. It's heaven!

We got ourselves sorted on the pitch. All our neighbours are either Dutch or German, tidy folk, so I am so glad we have this lovely motorhome and are not letting the side down with our old caravan. I feel quite grown-up with all the paraphernalia we have brought in the outdoor-furniture department – I even have tablecloths on this trip.

We headed to the pool. It's filled with sea water, as clean and blue as ever, but very salty and very buoyant. I was floating around on the water's surface, and it was quite difficult to swim – it was popping me up and out of the water bottom first, not a sight for sore eyes believe me!

For a late lunch I made myself a very quick meal from my recipe list: pasta puttanesca. Very delicious and, as I have yet to buy parmesan, I served it without cheese, so it was almost vegan (just a splash of Worcestershire sauce stopped it from being so if you omit that, it is vegan). John declined, and had a ham sandwich. As you know by now, he's not keen on pasta!

I spent the late afternoon just sitting and taking it all in. Counting my blessings again and strangely thinking about my dad. Dad was a veteran of the Italian campaign in World War II. He was called up in 1939 immediately after his 18th birthday and spent all the war in Italy. I guess he left as a boy

and returned as a man. I wish I had asked him more when I had the chance. I wonder many things, but firstly I wonder how on earth they got the troops here – well, he went right down to the heel of Italy and beyond, to Sicily. I assume it was in trucks, or it might have been on trains. It must have been both exciting and terrifying at the same time. I could investigate, as I'm sure there is information of this kind on the World Wide Web.

In the evening we decided to throw caution to the wind and eat out. The restaurant looked good and was busy. We dined outside and had pizza – it just had to be done, day one in Italy, eating some pizza! I enjoyed it. John's pizza had chips as a topping! He didn't eat his crusts – typical!

We had a minor fallout in the restaurant, as John was sick of taking photographs of me eating my pizza. I explained again about my book and how I need good-quality photographs to show what we've been doing. Anyway, he was adamant, so we came home in a bit of a huff. It was a bit of a dampener on the day, but it happened, and I will try to learn from that for tomorrow.

On the plus side, still 100 percent compliance on the swimming each day front. Buona notte.

– *Day 9 Recipe* –
SPAGHETTI PUTTANESCA

This popular pasta dish has a story to it. Legend has it that the prostitutes of Naples would make this meal between clients, as it was quick to make and is hearty enough to have kept them full of energy.

Ingredients (serves 2)

- 200g spaghetti *(see notes on measurements on page 22)*
- 2 tablespoons olive oil
- 1 onion, finely chopped
- 4 cloves garlic, crushed
- 400g can chopped tomatoes
- 1 tablespoon dried Italian herbs or oregano
- 2 tablespoons capers
- 2 tablespoons olives
- 1 tablespoon Worcestershire sauce *(or a few anchovies)*
- 1 teaspoon chilli flakes
- Salt and pepper
- Handful parmesan
- Fresh basil to garnish

Method

Fill a large pan with water, add a tablespoon of salt and bring it to the boil.

Add the spaghetti to the boiling water and follow the pack instructions, cooking until just 'al dente'.

Meanwhile, in a large frying pan, heat the oil and then cook the onions gently until they have softened. Add the garlic, continuing to cook for a minute, but taking care not to burn the garlic.

Add the herbs and the chopped tomatoes.

Cook for a few minutes and then add all the other ingredients and cook until the pasta is ready.

Add a few tablespoons of pasta water to the sauce. Drain (but do not rinse) the pasta and add it to the sauce.

Serve with a little parmesan cheese and a sprig of basil.

Everything
you see I owe
to spaghetti.

Sophia Loren

– *Day 10* –
SANREMO,
LIGURIA

The first full day in Italy is now under our belt, and it has been a good one, with not a single niggle or cross word – a few sighs of exasperation and rolled eyes, but not an actual complaint. Am I difficult to live with, Diary? Of course I am not – always full of the joys of spring and chilled out in temperament, that's me, ha, ha!

Anyway today, day 10 of 30, started literally at the crack of dawn. The dawn chorus is sung by some birds with strong lungs, and because of the heat we had our windows ajar. The chorus was as loud as any I have ever heard, and I decided to embrace the day and get up and go outside. I was not alone sitting watching the campsite still in slumber mode – one solitary Dutch man was outside his caravan reading, then a young woman in shorts and flip-flops appeared from the direction of the beach, likely getting in a shower before the rush hour in the sanitary block kicks in.

I discovered whilst sitting outside so early that the wifi works a little better at this time of day, but not well enough to transfer files. A message told me my 59 photos will take seven hours to transfer! I clicked on my mobile data, and they went flying off to the UK like a rocket – impressive.

John stirs, we press the button to tell our bed to levitate eerily into the ceiling, and our bedroom once again becomes a sitting room. John has a bowl of cornflakes, and we drink hot beverages – tea for me and coffee for him – and we wander off to look at the sea. I can see the sea from our motorhome through a gap in the palm trees, and it's so close. The little beach is lovely, a cove, and pebbly, but then I am not into sandcastle building anymore, so was not put off by that. There are what we think were gun emplacements built into the rocks, probably leftovers from the war I suppose. One man fishing, one small boat sailing, and that's it at seven this morning at the beach. Walking back, we discover a sunbathing platform with sunbeds and deckchairs, again belonging to the campsite and free to use. We take a seat and drink in the moment.

I saw a Lidl somewhere when we arrived yesterday, so we set off with my shopping bag and a rucksack to look. We couldn't find it; it must be further away than I thought, but we did find a Carrefour supermarket. It looked small from the outside, but like a Tardis, it was just massive inside. Oh joy upon joy, every aisle had treats for my eyes. A whole aisle dedicated to pasta, one for bread, one for condiments, wine and beer of course, fresh fish and seafood. The fruits and vegetables were a riot of colour, and there were cheeses, cakes, breadsticks, olives... I was so thrilled with the spectacle. I had been concerned that I might struggle to get ingredients in Italy, although I'm not sure why I would think that. I bought a few things, including a

small carton of amaretti biscuits to savour with coffee back at the motorhome – quite expensive, but they were the real deal and artisanal.

Back to the motorhome, and I made our lunch. This time the ham sandwich escaped John's clutches as I explained to him that I was making my recipe of the day for lunch. We were having bruschetta – grilled crusty bread, rubbed with garlic, drizzled with extra-virgin olive oil and then topped with fresh tomatoes and basil, or garlic mushrooms with parsley. Made in minutes, light enough for a filling lunch, and delicious, John agreed. Perhaps going forward, it'll be out with the ham sandwich and in with bruschetta? Somehow, I think not, but you never know. After letting lunch settle, we headed for the beach, carrying our camp chairs with us and a towel for me. Two groups of people were already there and had made a base camp. We settled ourselves and relaxed, which was easy to do. Just the sound of the gentle waves (no crashing waves in the Mediterranean) lapping at the shore and the screeching gulls lulling us into a meditative mode.

I had my swimming costume on, as I had decided today's swim was to be a sea swim. I made a right spectacle of myself

getting both in and out, the pebbles hurting my feet, and I only got wet when I became unbalanced and tipped in backwards. John, armed with his camera, was taking the most unflattering photos of the proceedings. I might decide to get on a diet, truth be told – it is sometimes when you catch a glimpse in these situations that you see yourself as you really are, in my case overweight. Anyway, forget all that, the sea was good, not cold at all and it was very invigorating. I floated around and swam for a bit before crawling on my hands and knees back up to the security of my beach towel.

Once back at the motorhome we had a siesta, as that early-morning start was telling on me. We lowered the bed and had 40 winks, a power nap, a snooze – call it what you will, but it did the trick. I was up and refreshed in no time. For dinner tonight we had leftovers. The fridge in the van is very good, large and has a freezer section too. I defrosted some chicken Provençal for John, and I had a portion of puttanesca pasta with added mushrooms and tomatoes from today's lunch. I treated John to some sauté potatoes, and he was a happy bunny, he is easy to please if I steer clear from his 'won't eat' list. Diary, let me tell you something. When I was due to get married to John, his mum gave me some tips about keeping him happy in the food department. He was 42 and still living at home, so he was quite set in his ways. She said: 'Our John likes a roast dinner on Sunday, leftover roast meat and chips on Monday, shepherd's pie on Tuesday, fish fingers on Wednesday…' and so on through the week, same routine every week. It has taken over 30 years to make the progress I have, but there's still room for improvement!

That's it, a good solid day, an early night once again, as we travel to Tuscany tomorrow. The first time I heard the word Tuscan it was on a can of soup, Tuscan bean. It was delicious and very healthy. That's why I am going to Tuscany, to make soup!

Goodnight.

– Day 10 Recipe –
BRUSCHETTA

Bruschetta (pronounced 'brusketa') is a popular starter or antipasti in Italy. Things on toast might be the easiest way to describe it, although that doesn't make it sound quite so fancy, so bruschetta it remains for this recipe. Good bread – usually a baguette, sliced – rubbed with garlic, lightly toasted, and then drizzled with oil before adding toppings of your choice. Anything goes really, but here I used tomatoes and mushrooms as my toppings.

Ingredients (serves 2)

Base

- Thick slices of white baguette
- 1 clove of garlic, peeled
- Extra-virgin olive oil

Toppings – tomato

- 2 large tomatoes, diced
- Sea salt
- Torn basil leaves
- Balsamic glaze or vinegar

Toppings – mushroom

- Olive oil
- 8 large mushrooms, thickly sliced
- 4 cloves of garlic, crushed
- Salt and pepper
- Squeeze lemon juice
- Chopped parsley
- Parmesan cheese *(optional)*

Method

To prepare the base, lightly toast the slices of bread and then rub them with garlic and drizzle over the extra-virgin olive oil.

Tomato toppings: Season the diced tomatoes very liberally with salt, and pile onto the toast. Add basil and a drizzle of balsamic glaze or vinegar.

Mushroom toppings: Heat oil in a frying pan, and sauté the mushrooms. Add the garlic, and cook for a minute, then season well with salt and pepper. Pile onto the bread and finish with a squeeze of lemon juice, parsley, and a little parmesan cheese.

*A woman who can
eat a real brushetta is
a woman you can love
and who can love you.*
Nick Harkaway

– *Day 11* –

– *Day 11* –
LAMPORECCHIO,
PISTOIA

We had an early call today, as we were bound for pastures new, Tuscany. I think I told you yesterday about my first introduction to Tuscany. Donkeys' years ago, when I was on yet another slimming regime, I discovered a can of soup that fit the bill in terms of calories and taste. I have always been partial to soup, ever since I was a child, but I had no idea that it could be made from scratch, easily and very cheaply. I am sure my mum never made any, as ours were always cans from the 57 varieties brand. Anyway, I digress. Since trying that bean soup and then watching lots of TV shows about Italian travel and food, I have had a desire to go to Tuscany. Today was the day I made it happen!

We left the site at Sanremo bang on 8:00am, and within five minutes I was already having an altercation with the same toll booth that I had met on the way in. Remember, Diary, I had to press that big red button? Same trying to go out – there we were puzzling as to why a ticket would not dispense automatically as they do in France. I started to get a bit anxious, then John said: 'Press the red knob.' If I were full of my normal wit and repartee, I may have made some sharp retort to that but, as it was, I just pressed the button and out popped a ticket. Thank goodness for that!

The journey was straightforward today, albeit quite long – about four and a half hours with many tunnels, one after the other. I swear even though it's along the coast, we saw more tunnels than sea. It made me think about how the Roman Empire got on marching along, or did they have boats and sail over to Marseille or somewhere similar, like the sophisticates they were? It proves to me how little general knowledge I have – I do okay in a pub quiz or playing Trivial Pursuit, but only in my favourite subjects, which are food and books. I think back to my school days and what aspects of geography and history we were taught. Sheep farming in Australia, coal mining in the UK, the formation of rivers and volcanoes in geography and the Napoleonic Wars and the Tudors in history. Nothing to answer my many questions on this trip!

We arrived at our chosen campsite intact. I say this because it was a rare old climb up to the top of, perhaps not quite a mountain, but a massive hill, and we are now perched on a plateau with panoramic views. The pool area is quite wonderful, obviously situated for the best aspect, and it truly is gorgeous. It has an infinity pool – you know, the ones where from a certain angle the water looks to go on into the horizon.

breaker. Once correctly attired in the millinery department, I went in for a splash about, on my own, not a soul to share the experience. To be fair, the site seems quiet, certainly compared to the last site we were at. After the swim, we had refreshments at the bar – John a beer and an ice cream cone for me. Very nice indeed, although it was a bit blowy up on the terrace, so we sheltered indoors. I could sense that there may be a storm brewing, and I was keen to return to the van and make the ribollita, the Tuscan bean soup.

I prepared the ingredients very quickly: the recipe is simple, and you can adjust the vegetables to include what you like or have in the fridge. The key components are the beans – a can of cannellini is what I used, but anything will do – and some stale bread. I didn't tell John that I had dunked in half of yesterday's baguette, as I thought knowing that would have

sent the soup onto his 'won't eat' list, but as it turned out, he liked it and I loved it. Definitely a winner! I was right about the storm too as, just after I had taken my soup photographs, the heavens opened and we quickly moved indoors to eat it.

We are both ready for an early night now Diary, but I want to tell you something exciting. We have got big plans whilst we're here in Tuscany. Tomorrow we are going to Vinci, a nearby town where the famous Leonardo grew up; the next day we are going to Florence; and the day after that I am having a cooking lesson in the kitchen here on the campsite. We'll be making something Italian, probably gnocchi, and I am thrilled at the prospect. I'm pleased to leave off the driving for a few days and see some of the local sights.

I just have to write up a few more notes on my laptop and then it's off to bed, another fabulous day under my belt.

I made my debut in this new pool wearing the compulsory swim cap. I mean, why? I feel self-conscious in my costume as it is without the added impact of a rubber helmet. I couldn't even get it on my head without some help from John, it was a right caper. Oh well, it had to be done, I am not a rule

– Day 11 Recipe –
RIBOLLITA

Beans are a common ingredient in Tuscan food and they feature in this popular regional soup. Unusually, ribollita also contains chunks of stale bread, so is a great dish for using up those ends of baguette that we often find we have hanging around. Historically, this is a peasant dish, including beans, bread and vegetables (it seems cavolo nero, or kale is always included if you can get hold of any, if not anything dark green, such as spinach, would work). I used tinned, chopped tomatoes and when I use tins, I often add a dollop of ketchup to sweeten them up a bit.

Ingredients (serves 2)

- 2 tablespoons olive oil
- 1 onion, finely chopped
- 1 carrot, finely diced
- 1 red pepper, chopped into small chunks
- 3 garlic cloves, crushed
- 1 tablespoon dried thyme or rosemary
- 1 teaspoon chilli flakes
- 1 tin of chopped tomatoes
- 1 tablespoon ketchup
- 1 litre vegetable stock *(made using a stock cube or stockpot)*
- 1 tin of cannellini beans
- 4 or 5 handfuls of leafy greens *(see note above)*
- 2 thick slices stale bread, broken into chunks
- Salt and pepper
- Parmesan cheese

Method

Heat the oil in a large pan. Add the onion, pepper and carrots to soften for a few minutes, then add all the ingredients except the leafy greens, bread, salt, and parmesan cheese. Bring to a boil and then reduce to a simmer until the carrots are soft and the volume has reduced by about half.

Add the leafy greens and cook for about 10 minutes. Finally, add the bread. Season to taste and scatter the parmesan cheese on the top.

Everyday happiness means you can't wait to come home because the soup is hot.

George Burns

Today has been a great day. I woke up very early once again and saw the sunrise from my bed, the Italian birds were singing, and it occurred to me once again how fortunate I am to be enjoying all these things. It is all too easy to take things for granted and not appreciate the full glory of your surroundings. Phew, that's got the day's diary entry off onto a philosophical vibe, but hey I feel it, so I write it, warts and all. Fortunately we were wart-free today.

John discovered that his cornflake box was empty. Now Diary, as you well know by now, John is very much a creature of habit and knows what he likes to have at mealtimes. Breakfast is always cereal: cornflakes in summer, Weetabix in spring and autumn, and porridge in winter. The quandary was what to do. I dispatched him off to the campsite shop to buy bread and jam. After a false start, when he returned to check

with me which bread he should buy, giving me some funny descriptions of what he had seen on offer, and finally returned with a couple of what I think were focaccia teacakes. No jam to be had though, so it was bread and cheese for breakfast, and it was very good too.

The campsite here is very well organised and, as it is quite remote up that hill/mountain on a plateau, they have a shuttle-bus service to take guests to various local places to enable them to see the delights of the area. Today we had booked the shuttle to take us to Vinci – the town where Leonardo da Vinci had grown up (his name literally means Leonardo from Vinci). It was only a 10-minute drive in the bus, but the lady driving us was brilliant and chatted the whole way, pointing out things of interest and giving us a low-down on da Vinci's background.

Seemingly, he had been born out of wedlock and was brought up by his father's family who were well known and quite prosperous. Little is known of his mother. He was given a basic education in the town of Vinci where he lived with his grandfather. They spotted in him a talent for drawing, and he went off to Florence to develop his skills. He was a genius. We visited the museums in the town and saw all the different things that he had worked on and invented. It was totally fascinating, unbelievable really. After taking our time at the museums and viewing points, which were totally stunning as we could look way out over the Tuscan landscape, we went to find a bite to eat.

We found a small roadside restaurant and got ourselves settled at a table for two. It was busy with Italian families, all talking with passion nineteen to the dozen, about what of course I had no idea. We ordered bruschetta, as I wanted to compare the real deal with the ones I made a few days ago. Equally nice, but very similar is how I would rate them, enjoyed with a beer for John and a bitter lemon for me. John ordered a cheesecake and we both had one of those microscopic coffees.

After lunch we went into the church where da Vinci had been baptised. I lit a candle and sent up a thank you to the universe for all my blessings. It was very serene and cool in the church, and it felt good to sit and be quiet for a few minutes. When we came out of the church, we could hear rumbles of thunder, the sky looked dark and ominous, so we hurried to a bar and ordered another drink to keep us dry, and we just sat and watched as the heavy drops of rain splattered down outside.

With our trip to Vinci over, we caught our shuttle back to the campsite, by which time the sun was out and l decided to go for my swim. I managed to get the wretched swim cap on my head and in I went. It was even more glorious than yesterday, as the breeze had dropped and it was warm and just gorgeous; sadly it was turfing out time (being almost 7 in the evening) and the pool guy came to tell me I had 10 minutes left.

It was dinner time, so I hurried back and made dinner number 12 of 30. Tonight it was a favourite, Tuscan chicken, also called Marry Me Chicken. It is chicken breast cooked with spices and herbs, sundried tomatoes, cream and parmesan cheese. It's a fiery red colour and goes well with rice, which I served for myself, but I made some potatoes for John. I indulge him sometimes!

The band was tuning up at the site, which we could hear it from the motorhome. We decided to stroll to the bar, have a drink and listen to the band. It was quite late, already past my normal bedtime, but it did feel good, sitting watching the sun go down, listening to half-decent music and drinking a stunning Aperol spritz.

It was a good day, diary! Buenos noches. (Wait, isn't that Spanish?)

– Day 12 Recipe –
TUSCAN CHICKEN

This dish has the nickname Marry Me Chicken as it is said to be so delicious that if you serve it to your sweetheart, a marriage proposal will follow! We all know that Italy is a very passionate and romantic country so be careful who you make this for!

Ingredients (serves 2)

- 1 tablespoon olive oil and a knob of butter
- 2 chicken breasts, sliced thinly on the horizontal to create thinner slices
- Handful of mushrooms, sliced
- Two garlic cloves, crushed
- 1 tablespoon tomato purée
- 1 tablespoon smoked paprika
- 1 tablespoon dried oregano
- 1 teaspoon chilli flakes
- 200ml chicken stock
- Half a jar of sundried tomatoes
- 100ml double cream
- Handful of parmesan cheese

Method

Heat the oil and butter together in a large frying pan. Brown the chicken in the pan on both sides until it is golden, then remove to a plate.

Cook the mushrooms and garlic together, along with all the herbs and spices and the tomato purée.

Add the chicken stock and simmer until the volume is reduced by about half.

Return the chicken to the pan and add the sundried tomatoes. Cook for a further 10 minutes or so, then add the cream and the cheese.

Garnish with parsley and serve with mashed potatoes, rice or pasta.

My weaknesses have always been food and men, in that order.

Dolly Parton

— Day 13 —

LAMPORECCHIO,
PISTOIA

Diary, today was a bit of a culture vulture day, as this morning we went to Florence. To get there, we took advantage of the shuttle bus from the campsite, and they ferried us to the local station where we took the train into Florence. The train itself was a double-decker and quite full. I was watching a group of six Italian youths – teenagers – and they were so animated and joyful, quite the opposite of the stereotypical teenager. Mind you, there is no saying they were like that in their own homes, but out for a day, presumably in a gang of pals, they were a joy to behold, something quite innocent about them and on the cusp of adulthood, their whole lives yet to unfurl.

not thin and crispy this time, more of a deep pan, and sat outside to devour. Of course, as in any city there are street vendors roaming around trying to tempt you to buy their wares. In Florence, the accessory of the day was a selfie stick. I must have declined about half-a-dozen times; I do have a selfie stick anyway, but it has never seen the light of day, and to be frank I would feel a bit silly walking around with one. There were people begging too, and one chap indicated he would like some pizza, so I offered the tray, and he selected pepperoni over the meatball one. I guess he is the local expert on toppings!

Arriving in Florence was a bit of a jolt to the senses. I expected the usual mad flurry around a big railway station, but once outside, in the blistering heat, I felt a bit overwhelmed by the sheer number of human beings that were teeming all around us, many pulling along suitcases. I took some photos of our location, as we needed to be sure we could find our way back later. Armed with a tourist map, off we went, and within five minutes we started to see those stunning, captivating sights. So remarkable and beautiful. I guess over the centuries there have been thousands of people trying to capture the glory of Florence in words, so I shall not even begin to put in my two penn'orth. Suffice to say we were captivated, bowled over by the sheer majesty of it all.

Due to an early start today, I had skipped breakfast and I was soon feeling very peckish. We found an exceedingly small shop selling pizza by the kilo – there were tables outside and we were tempted by the trays of pizza that we could see people eating. We bought a couple of slabs,

Full to the brim with carbs, I felt a bit more energetic, and we continued to navigate the streets. I was fascinated outside Hermès, the designer-scarf shop, to see a queue of people waiting for a very smart door attendant to let them in. Every minute or two, in would go another couple of people, although I didn't see anyone coming out. The shops were all very smart but, not being a shopper, I just wandered past, seeking the cooler, darker side streets.

We didn't try to buy tickets for the museums and the churches. The queues were ridiculous, and I think I would have suffered too much standing for such a long time. There were crocodiles of people being led along the pavements by tour guides, and they were always on the shady side of the street, many with parasols or huge brimmed sunhats. They didn't give way to anyone coming at them from the opposite direction – how rude! It occurred to me though, that I would like to return to Florence in the future as part of an organised tour, so I could find out more and visit some of the fabulous places we saw today.

We found ourselves by the river. Ah, some longed-for shade, drinks, and some garden furniture to relax and while away a little time. We sat for about an hour, and John fell asleep. Once or twice I had to double check he hadn't expired due to the heat, but fortunately he was just having a quick 40 winks.

towards Rome or Naples, as it was difficult to be sure which platform and then which train. We managed it though, and within half an hour we were back in the sanctuary of the countryside. I was desperate for a shower when I got back to the motorhome. I was like some sort of whirling dervish, casting off my sweaty

clothes and grabbing my towel and shower gel, and almost running to the sanitary block. After a busy, hot day, I needed it, and felt tons better for it.

It was quite late in the day to be cooking, but I had planned a quick dinner for this evening. Today's recipe was a cheat's 'wrap' pizza. I know, pizza again but, whilst in Italy it must be done, as many times as possible in a day! It is a very easy dish, using a tortilla wrap as the base, some ketchup for the sauce, and then cheese, spinach and an egg to top. It took only a matter of 10 minutes before it was on the table. As I was preparing the table outside for the photoshoot of the dish (passing campers often make comments), three motorbikes with leather-clad German riders arrived at the pitch next to us. They stripped off their leathers (I wasn't peeping, promise!) and set to work erecting their tents, and in only a few minutes they were done and settled, quick work indeed.

I had a couple of glasses of wine, and John had some beers before we settled down for bed. Another good day, although I have weary bones now and am looking forward to uninterrupted sleep. Who knows if those Germans next door are snorers, but I shall soon find out. Hush to the birds too, tone down the volume on tomorrow morning's chorus please, just this once!

Thus, refreshed and rested, we made our way back through the crowds, dodging the crocodiles of tourists, and successfully, with the help of the phone sat-nav, made it to the station. It was a bit of a hairy experience, and I was quite anxious that we would get on the wrong train and find ourselves hurtling

See you in the morning!

– Day 13 Recipe –

'IT'S A WRAP' PIZZA FLORENTINE

This is a bit of a cheat's way to make something very close to pizza. If you only have a hob, making pizza is a challenge. I discovered that by using a tortilla wrap, a pizza is quite possible, especially as authentic pizzas have a thin, crispy base!

A Florentine pizza always includes egg and spinach. I cheated with the egg by frying it separately and placed it on to the pizza once both pizza and egg were cooked.

The same method can be used to make any other 'wrap' pizza you fancy.

Ingredients (serves 1)

- Spray oil
- Large tortilla wrap
- 1 tablespoon ketchup or pesto
- Grated mozzarella cheese
- Couple handfuls of fresh spinach
- 1 tablespoon dried oregano
- Salt and pepper
- Parmesan cheese
- 1 egg

Method

Spray a lidded frying pan with oil. Put on a moderate heat, and place the wrap in the pan and cook on both sides to soften.

Spread the ketchup or pesto on the wrap, leaving margin of a couple of centimetres all round. Lay the cheese on the base and scatter with oregano. Lay the spinach on the cheese, add salt and pepper, and then cover with the lid. Be careful to keep on a moderate heat to avoid burning the base.

Cook a fried egg separately.

When the cheese is melted and the spinach wilted, place the egg on the top and scatter with parmesan.

Keep calm and order pizza.
Tiger Woods

– Day 14 –
LAMPORECCHIO,
PISTOIA

Hey Diary, **what a delicious day** it's been today. Day 14 already, two whole weeks of you I and on this fabulous trip together, and John makes three, so a bit of a 'ménage à trois'. I say delicious, because I ate some tasty things, but also because I have had a deliciously decadent, relaxing time. I indulged myself in the luxury of an afternoon doing nothing but sitting, swimming and snoozing.

I must make a confession before I go any further, I forgot to mention in yesterday's entry that I had missed a day's swim. This was unintentional, but by the time I got back from the day out in Florence, the pool had closed for the day. I was a bit miffed, as I felt I had let myself down, but I gave myself a talking to and put it into perspective. I try to learn that I can't control every small thing and to go with the flow, just like last week when my sandals floated down the river Ardèche after we capsized – they came back to me and it was all fine in the end.

Anyway, today I made up for it a bit and had two swims in the pool, and I was sporting a new swimming cap, a red one that I bought at the shop here. No more squeezing my head into that awful rubber cap I was wearing the other day. I want to buy another swimming costume too, something bold and bright, possibly red, and I shall be on the lookout at our next campsite.

This morning was a lot of fun. I had booked myself on to a cooking class being held here at the campsite in Tuscany. It turned out to be more of a demonstration, with a couple of turns at being hands-on during the proceedings. The chef showed a small group of us how to make pasta – no machines to roll the dough, just a wooden rolling pin. First, she showed us how to prepare the dough by putting the flour onto a board, making a well in it and cracking five eggs into the well – a bit like I do when making Yorkshire pudding batter, but of course

I use a bowl for that. She then beat the eggs, pulling in a little flour a bit at a time, before adding some water and mixing everything until it came together into a kneadable dough. We all had a turn at kneading the dough. Next, she started to roll the dough until it wrapped right onto the rolling pin and repeated this over and over. To cut the pasta, we used a cutting contraption made from a wooden box with very fine wire strung across (like a huge egg slicer – John likes to slice his hard-boiled eggs this way). We laid a sheet of pasta onto the wires and then rolled the pin over the top so the pasta was cut by the wires and dropped into the box beneath in very fine strings.

The chef went off to cook some of it for us to taste. In only a matter of minutes she was back with a steaming platter of pasta coated with melted butter, sprinkled with parmesan and garnished with fresh sage. It was marvellous, so different. We were all given a Tupperware box with some uncooked pasta to take with us. We were also shown the herb garden, and encouraged to take whatever we wanted, so we did, most of us choosing sage. It was a fabulous experience and I had a great time.

As I already mentioned, the afternoon was spent down at the pool. I struggle sometimes with just laying still, basking in the sun, as I get a bit restless. Today, I closed my eyes and listened. It's amazing how much more you hear when you are not distracted by what you can see. All around there were different things to tune in to: water, birds, rustling of leaves, children's voices, the hum of a strimmer somewhere. I heard the crunch of wheels, and I opened my eyes to see a young woman coming along pushing a rather stately old-fashioned pram. It made me think back to when my babies were born. The advice back then was to put the baby in a pram and put them outside so they could sleep in the fresh air. The books said in any weather, rain or shine, but to remember to put a cat net over if you left the pram unattended. I wonder if people still do that anymore, I somehow doubt it.

After these musings I had my swim and a read, and managed to have a nap. Tomorrow, we move to a new campsite, so I want to be as rested as possible, and it has been a busy couple of days doing the culture stuff – it has taken it out of me!

John's been OK. He doesn't like sitting around swimming pools, so he wandered off to take a walk and had a beer. He is contented now, getting into the groove and doing his daily tasks. He is responsible for some of the motorhome maintenance, like refilling the water tank, emptying the loo and the waste water and dealing with the garbage. He knows his place!

For tonight's meal I had pasta planned. I won't bore you again with John and his dislike of pasta; however, in this morning's class when urged to taste a sample of the pasta by the chef, John (not being a rude person) had some and concurred that it was very nice. John ate tonight's dish, made with the fresh pasta, without complaint, so a big tick on that score. I served the pasta along with spinach, sundried tomatoes, cream, mushrooms, cheese and some of the fresh sage from the herb garden.

Diary, I have had a lovely time here on this campsite in Tuscany, we have seen some truly remarkable things and met some charming, warm and friendly people. In some ways I will be sad to leave, but I'm also looking forward to moving on.

Night for now, must get my head down, I need some sleep!

– Day 14 Recipe –
FLORENTINE PASTA

I developed this pasta dish as I was determined to get more spinach in my Tuscan recipes! There are many Florentine-style dishes hailing from the Tuscan city of Florence and they often include spinach. I made this dish in just one pot in around 20 minutes. I used sundried tomato pesto, as I had a jar with me, but it's easy to substitute a little tomato purée and sundried tomatoes if you have them. Omit the salami if you want to stay vegetarian for this one.

Ingredients (serves 2)

- 2 tablespoons olive oil
- 1 onion, chopped
- 1 red pepper, chopped
- Handful of mushrooms, sliced
- 4 cloves garlic, crushed
- 1 tablespoon dried oregano
- Salt and pepper
- 200g dried pasta
- 750ml stock
- 2 tablespoons sundried tomato pesto *(or see note above)*
- About 10 slices of salami
- Handful of grated mozzarella cheese
- 4 handfuls of spinach
- 100ml double cream
- Sprinkle of parmesan
- Torn basil or sage leaves for garnish

Method

In a large frying pan, heat the oil and cook off the onions for a few minutes. Add the peppers, mushrooms, garlic and oregano. Cook this for a few minutes and then add salt and pepper.

Pour in the stock and the pasta. Bring to the boil and then simmer until the pasta is cooked and the stock is reduced.

Add the sundried tomato pesto, the cheese and the spinach. Allow the spinach to wilt and then stir through the cream mixing everything well.

Serve and sprinkle parmesan and fresh basil or sage on the top.

After a good dinner one can forgive anybody, even one's own relatives.

Oscar Wilde

– Day 15 –

CA' SAVIO,
VENICE

We have been on the move again today, Diary, from one side of Italy to the other. Before we left Tuscany this morning, we had a lovely breakfast sitting and taking in the panoramic views for one last time. When I went down to the shop to buy some bread and milk for the journey, I had a very nice surprise. The chef that had led the pasta class that I attended yesterday was floating about. She was quite excited, talking to me in rapid staccato Italian, but I think I got the gist. She was keen for me to get her photograph in a magazine article that I am writing a piece for – she even presented me with a bottle of wine as a gift, or was it a bribe?! I said that I would do what I could, in my best broken Italian, and off I went.

We made our way back down the twisting and narrow roads and quickly found the autoroute – well, the sat-nav did, good old Sally! – heading towards Venice, initially in the direction of Bologna. Passing through the mountains, which were very dark green and totally covered in trees, I remarked how beautiful it was. Even more so when we found ourselves on a 'touristique' section, and very strangely, for a while there was not another vehicle to be seen. Making good progress, we approached Bologna, and I challenged John with a cooking question: I asked which popular meal originated in Bologna.

He got it right in one: 'Spag bol' says he. I then proceed to tell him for the umpteenth time how I remember making my first ever spaghetti bolognaise. Shall I tell you, Diary?

decent progress, and after almost four hours we reached our destination – Ca' Savio on the Adriatic coast. We have been to this area before, back in the day when not just John and I worked for a camping holiday company, but both our daughters did too. They were both based out here on the Adriatic, so we visited them a couple of times one season. I knew it was a bucket-and-spade-type resort and was looking forward to the contrast from the other sites we have been to so far on this trip.

When I was a child, we often had spaghetti on toast I never questioned what spaghetti was or how it was made. I just knew it came in tins that Mum bought from the shop, and the label stressing 'Do not overheat, as it will impair the flavour' – I used to enjoy reading everything and anything, including food labels and the backs of cereal boxes, but I digress... In 1977, I was about 19 and an Italian restaurant sprung up in Leeds. It was called Bibis (it is still there today) and everyone locally was suddenly mad for Italian food. Soon I discovered that you could buy dried spaghetti (in very long packets) in the supermarket. My friend Susan came to my house, and we had a go at making 'spag bol'. It was a bit of a performance, and we overdid the ingredients, putting in random things like Oxo cubes, but it was exciting discovering this 'foreign' food and I can recall it very clearly.

Diary, thank you for bearing with that story, as I like to travel down memory lane from time to time. Back to the journey though. The landscape started to change, we lost the mountains, and things became flat and quite dry-looking by comparison. The roads we quite empty, so we made

We arrived at 2.00pm and the young man on the gate explained that there was a quiet period between 1.00pm and 3.00pm when vehicles were not allowed to drive about. We could park and hook up, and he would show us a choice of pitches and then perhaps, he suggested, we could get a drink at the bar. We did as he suggested, enjoyed a little ride with him on the golf buggy, selected our pitch and went to the bar and ordered some beer.

Once we were allowed access, we were settled in no time. That is one of the good things about motorhome travel, within minutes you are in holiday mode. Our pitch is great: large, shaded but with a bit of sun, water and electricity on the pitch, and about two minutes' walk to the beach.

What a glorious beach it is too. I decided today's swim would involve the sea. The sand was soft and golden, not a pebble to be had. I managed to enter the water with a modicum of grace, mind you I went in in shorts and T-shirt which is a tad more flattering to my bumpy and billowing figure. I loved the swim – the seawater was warm and it was just like wading into a bath. The water was so clear and clean, with nothing to be concerned about and no manky seaweed or detritus to get tangled up in.

Now I must mention the showers in the sanitary block... After my dip in the briny, I went for a shower. Oh bliss, cubicles with not only a shower and sink, but a loo too – like your very own bathroom. I have a bit of a thing about using public toilets. I know quite a few women share this, and it is almost a phobia for me. I just don't really like to use them, but somehow, here with this private set up, it feels different and so much better. John didn't understand when I explained this to him, as he will go into any loo anywhere, armed with a loo roll, and not bat an eye. Is it a man thing?

Tonight's recipe, number 15 of 30, is a quickie. Store-cupboard tuna pasta. Nothing fresh, not even an onion, so a perfect quick fix. Of course, John not only doesn't really like pasta, he doesn't like tuna either, but I thought it was very tasty. John

did eat it, but with bad grace, and I got annoyed with him then, so I went off for a walk to put a bit of space between us.

I reminded myself during my walk around the site to try to be kinder. I keep slipping up with that intention. I said at the start of the trip I wanted to be a kinder person, as well as to swim each day (I am doing OK with the swimming at least!). When I got back to the pitch I saw John's figure in the distance heading to the beach, looking for me. I caught up with him, he took my hand and we made friends. All is well with my world once more.

Good night, Diary, sleep well…

– Day 15 Recipe –

STORE-CUPBOARD TUNA PASTA

Not especially Venetian, although Venetians do eat a lot of fish. This is a complete store-cupboard dinner which is so fast to make, all done in the time it takes to cook the pasta. I used macaroni so it took six minutes! A perfect meal when you need food fast.

Ingredients (serves 2)

- 1.5 cups dried pasta
- 1 tablespoon sea salt
- 2 tablespoons extra-virgin olive oil
- Squeeze of garlic purée, or teaspoon garlic powder *(or fresh)*
- 1 teaspoon chilli flakes
- 2 tablespoons capers
- 1 tablespoon oregano
- 1 tablespoon Worcestershire sauce
- 1 can of tuna
- 1 carton of passata
- Salt and pepper

Method

Boil a large pan of water and add salt. Add the pasta and cook for as long as the packet instructions suggest.

Meanwhile, in a frying pan, warm the oil and cook the garlic, chilli flakes, oregano, Worcestershire sauce and capers for a few minutes. Drain the tuna and add it to the pan, breaking it up and mixing well. Add the passata and stir it well. Keep on a gentle heat until the pasta is cooked.

Drain the pasta, reserving one cup of the pasta water. Add a little of the reserved water to the tuna sauce and stir. Add the cooked pasta, adding more pasta water to loosen the sauce if required.

This is good eaten cold too, as a pasta salad!

People should always have a good bottle of extra virgin olive oil, a packet of pasta, tinned tomatoes and a good cheese somewhere in the fridge.

Gino D'Acampo

— Day 16 —
CA' SAVIO,
VENICE

Another day under our belt now Diary, I can't believe we are over halfway through our journey together. I wasn't going to use the cliché about time flying and all that, but it does, and I have used it. Today has been a non-travelling day, as we are staying three nights at Ca' Savio and today was the first full day here. I am starting to find a pattern of what suits us now, in terms of driving days and how long to stay on each site, and three nights is about right before my feet start itching to be on the move again.

This morning I discovered there was a farmers' market in a small town called Treporti. Being in the motorhome means we need to use public transport, hire a bike, or simply walk. Bikes and I are a thing of the past, although I will remind anyone that will listen that I once cycled 100 miles in one day! Yes, you heard correctly. I was sweet 16 and as fit as a butcher's dog back then. I was with my first husband, and we travelled from Featherstone to Ambleside and stayed in a youth hostel with separate dormitories for women and men – I remember not liking that aspect very much.

Anyway, back to getting to the market. After a breakfast of boiled eggs, fresh bread and coffee, we went to reception and we discovered that you need to buy tickets before getting on a bus anywhere. We bought our tickets from there and headed off to try to find the correct bus stop. We found a bus stop, a bus arrived, we hopped on, and I asked, 'Treporti'? 'No' says the driver, we hop off again, 'Madame' says the driver,

indicating we hop on again, so we do. Then he says: 'Five minutes, I change bus'. Oh, thinks I, he means get off and a different bus will come in five minutes, so I hop off again. 'No!', says the driver, 'Come', indicating we get on again! This time we get on and stay on, with no idea what was going to happen next, but we were glad of the air-conditioning, so I thought, you know what, let's go with the flow. What he meant was that we had been standing at the bus stop on the wrong side of the road. Ha, ha, a typical tourist mistake! We sat on the bus, he took us with him to the terminus, and then he turned the bus around and off we headed in the correct direction.

There were more issues with getting to the market, involving a second bus and a family from Ireland who were questioning me about the quality of the market and whether there were going to be any stalls to interest their four teenage children. I explained it was a farmers' market and, unless they were into fruit, veg and farm machinery, possibly not! However, as it turned out they may have liked it, as most of the stalls sold clothing, shoes and even yapping clockwork dogs. I skirted these, on the prowl for fruit-and-veg stalls, but one clothing stall caught my eye with its display of bright green ladies' wear. I was hoping to find a new swimming costume, but no beachwear was to be seen.

I found some food stalls and had a good old ogle at the wares on offer. Beautiful produce, bright colours, all glistening and

fresh-looking, and the strawberries were so red and inviting. I managed to sneak a few photographs. The bus journey home was more straightforward, and I think when we try to get to Venice tomorrow, we will know the ropes and have less hassle.

Once back at the campsite, we went to hire a bike for John, which cost 10 euros for a day, very good value. The man wheeled out one of those sit-up-and-beg-style bikes with a basket on the front. I nearly burst my sides laughing, you should have seen John's face. John is not a 'new man' in any sense of the word, and riding a bike with a shopping basket,

well, he wouldn't be seen dead doing that! I managed to explain to the man, who then wheeled out a much more suitable bicycle – a mountain bike. John was sorted and off we went for a bit of lunch. In the afternoon, I needed to spend a bit of quality time with making some notes of things to write and tell you about, Diary. John went off on his bike and left me to get up to date with things with a nice glass of wine.

I had read that there was an aqua-zumba class at 5.00pm in one of the swimming pools, though I wanted to go and have my daily dip in the pool at the same time. John and

I went, and we couldn't find a sun bed, as all of them were reserved with towels, so we perched on a step and watched the proceedings. A young lady was demonstrating the zumba moves from the poolside, and the folk in the pool were following her, music blaring. It was fun to watch, but I didn't join in. Instead, I had a discreet swim about at the opposite end of the pool, the water refreshing and not too chilly.

When I was drying off sitting next to John, I took a selfie of us both, a rare shot that looked quite nice – we looked happy and relaxed. I asked John which campsite he liked the most so far on the trip (we are on number seven) and it was quite sad, because he said he could only really remember the most recent one. We have to accept things and look for the positives – he is living in the moment and we're having a very good time.

To jolly us up a bit, I suggested we got an ice cream. We had a two-scoop cone each. John is a vanilla man through and through, but with a tiny bit of persuasion this time he tried one scoop vanilla and one scoop strawberry, a breakthrough indeed! I had chocolate and tiramisu, absolutely divine.

It seems a long entry this one, but I still have things to say! I set to work preparing meal number 16 of 30. I had intended to use the gas BBQ, but we learnt that they are not allowed, due to how dry it is here. I had marinated some chicken breasts earlier in the day, and I griddled these and served them with my Venetian potatoes – easy to make and very tasty. Big thumbs up from John, and not a scrap left on his plate.

After we had eaten, I heard what I thought was some sort of tractor that might have been cleaning the beach. I was wrong, it was a vehicle trawling up and down the campsite spraying everything with mosquito repellent. I had been nibbled lots of times already – it always happens doesn't it? Just when you have started to look good and healthy, with the glow of a suntan, ouch, bites, lumps and bumps and itches to spoil the look. Do mosquitoes have a purpose other than being very annoying I wonder?

Well Diary, with that thought, I'll say goodnight. We are hoping to go to Venice tomorrow. I want to be up and away to beat the crowds if possible, so wish us luck getting there!

MARINATED CHICKEN AND VENETIAN POTATOES

Cicchetti are bar snacks that are served in this area. The Italian equivalent of tapas. Anything small and savoury can be served but the one that caught my eye was the Venetian potatoes. This larger portion is a great side to a steak or maybe some smoked fish. Here I pair it with grilled chicken. Very easy to make and of course very moreish!

Ingredients (serves 2)

Venetian Potatoes

- 2 large baking-sized potatoes, unpeeled and cut into dice
- 1 onion, sliced
- 1 teaspoon smoked paprika
- 200ml chicken or vegetable stock
- Handful of grated cheese
- Salt and pepper

Marinated Chicken

- 2 chicken breasts
- 4 tablespoons white wine vinegar
- 2 tablespoons extra-virgin olive oil
- 1 teaspoon garlic
- 1 teaspoon Dijon mustard
- 2 teaspoons honey
- 1 teaspoon dried oregano

Method – Venetian Potatoes

Put the potatoes into a pan of salted water and bring to the boil. Boil for about five minutes and then drain and leave to cool. Wait until the par-boiled potatoes are cold before the next step, or they will break.

Heat the oil in a frying pan and sauté the potatoes until they are taking on a golden colour. Add the onions and lower the heat to cook the onions until they are soft and sticky. Sprinkle over the smoked paprika and stir well. Add the stock and simmer until the potatoes have absorbed all the stock.

Add the grated cheese and mix well to melt. Season to taste.

Method – Marinated Chicken

Mix all the marinade ingredients together and pour into a bag or container, then add the chicken. Leave in the fridge for a few hours to marinate.

Grill the chicken on a BBQ or in a frying pan, until the chicken is cooked through, for about 15 minutes, turning frequently.

Serve with the Venetian potatoes.

BBQ might not be the road to world peace but it's a start.

Anthony Bourdain

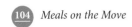

- *Day 17* -
CA' SAVIO,
VENICE

It was a red-letter day today, Diary, I got to Venice! It was surprisingly easy to get there from this campsite. Now that John and I are up to speed with how the buses work in Italy, we are on a roll. We just bought tickets from the campsite reception to get us to Punta Sabbioni, where we hopped on a boat to take us over the water to Venice and, just like that, we were there. The cost of the bus tickets was 5 euros and the boat 15 euros and I thought that 40 euros all-in for two people was pretty good value. In fact, I have been surprised by how reasonably priced food, drink and treats like ice creams are in Italy.

What a joy then, what a soaring and excited heart I had this morning, as we approached the harbour and were treated to that vista of the famous skyline of beautiful buildings set against the bluest of skies. Armed with a piece of advice from Vanessa, who had messaged me to say: 'Enjoy Venice, Mum, but if you feel a bit stressed, find a quiet and cool church to sit in.' I think she assumed that the streets would be a throng of tourists, like Florence a few days ago, but it was just perfect, not too busy at all, perhaps because we caught one of the early boats. So there's my top tip if you intend to visit, get up early and be on the first sailing.

I have been intrigued by the notion of Venice ever since I was 11 in 1969, and I moved up to high school in Pontefract. Our neighbour, Miss Winnifred Smith, gave me the book she had been awarded at the same school when she was a pupil there in 1916: *The Complete Works of William Shakespeare*. Battered even then, I tried to read it, bit by bit, but I was rather overwhelmed, and the 16th-century language defeated me. However, I did discover *The Merchant of Venice*, and became fascinated. My daughter, Vanessa, has the book now amongst her collection of old books.

We immediately headed up one of the small streets to find some shade, as the heat was blistering already. Immediately I was captivated by the things that I was seeing as we walked along – looking up there was laundry hanging between the buildings, and some buildings were maybe only a metre wide in places.

Cool and quiet courtyards tucked away, the mortar between the ancient red bricks missing from ground level up to about waist height – flooding from the canals causing the erosion perhaps? Quite soon, and it took me by complete surprise, we saw our

first small bridge and then our first canal and, as we stood atop the bridge, our first gondola and gondolier! Oh Diary, I was so thrilled, and I still am as I write these words. I hope this memory lasts forever, or at least until I visit again, which I will!

On and on we went, padding along the small streets, now wider and lined with shops selling beautiful wares – Murano glass, and masks and costumes for balls for the most part. I gazed through the shop windows in wonder at the food on sale – cannoli, meringues, marzipan fruits – and then the trattoria with their blackboards offering so many delights.

We headed for St Mark's Square, which was totally awesome. It was quite busy, especially the queues for the Basilica, but manageable nonetheless. It was too hot for me to linger for long, and we decided to get a cold drink and some lunch. We got lucky and found a small bar with a table for two right outside. There were cicchetti on offer in the window. Cicchetti are small snacks, often things on bread, just bite-sized and a bit like meze or tapas.

So here we were in a bar, faced with a choice of which cicchetti to choose. The guy behind the bar explained each of the toppings to me, and I liked the sound of all of them except the last one, which looked lovely but involved octopus. I selected six different ones, ordered drinks, and went and joined John outside to relax and enjoy.

After lunch I remembered I wanted to see the Bridge of Sighs. This was the name given by Lord Byron as the translation from the Italian 'Ponte dei sospiri'. The bridge is connected to the prison, and legend has it that the prisoners would look out from the bridge and sigh at their final view of the city before being taken to their cells. We found it, took the photographs, and continued our wandering around the myriad small, fascinating streets. I did ask John if we could go on a gondola ride, but he balked at the cost, 80 euros for half an hour. I didn't push it, but that is fast becoming a regret.

Our day in Venice was coming to an end, and we were waiting for the boat back. We decided to sit on the harbour-front and order a drink. I still felt a bit excited about being in Venice, so I ordered a Campari spritz, just to enjoy the vibrant colour as much as its rather bitter taste, which I somehow both like and dislike at the same time. It came in a rather beautiful glass which made it even more perfect for the occasion.

Once back at the campsite, we decided to swim together. Bonded by such a great day in Venice, we felt rather revitalised, and we splashed about in that warm sea like a couple of 'young uns'. John's almost 76, but you would never think it, he is so lean and looks years younger.

Back at the motorhome I made polpette with polenta. Polpette are meatballs, though tonight I just scrunched up some sausages

to make mine. Polenta is a new thing for us – cornmeal mixed with water and brought to a boil. John likes it – I think because it resembles mashed potatoes – so it's another winner of a meal, which seals this as a perfect day for me.

Hang on a minute. As I am writing this, I've just heard something and seen a flash – could it be a change in the weather? It is, I am going to stop writing and watch...

It's half an hour later and I have been watching what John calls an electric storm, with lots of sheet-lightning. It was quite exciting seeing the skyline over the sea light up. I played some 'summer of the sixties' music on my phone as I watched, and it was fabulous. A great end to a top day.

Moving on tomorrow, Lake Garda calls!

– Day 17 Recipe –
POLPETTE AND POLENTA

This dish is so simple and extremely scrumptious.
Polpette are small meatballs and polenta is cornmeal that you mix with boiling water. I made the meatballs using sausages – any will do, but ideally use spiced Italian ones. You can follow my method for the polenta, or cook it according to the packet instructions, but it is important to add copious amounts of butter and parmesan cheese to ensure maximum creaminess and taste.

Ingredients (serves 2)

Polpette
- 6 sausages
- Oil
- One onion, chopped
- About 8 mushrooms, thickly sliced
- 4 garlic cloves, crushed
- 2 large fresh tomatoes, thickly sliced
- Splash of balsamic vinegar
- Splash of red wine *(optional)*
- 2 tablespoons tomato purée
- 1 tablespoon dried oregano
- Splash of water
- Salt and pepper
- Fresh parsley/basil for garnish

Polenta
- 1 cup of quick cook polenta *(fine)*
- 4 cups of cold water
- Teaspoon salt
- Large knob of butter
- Handful of parmesan

Method

Squeeze the sausage meat out of the skins and roll into meatballs about the size of a walnut. Heat oil in a frying pan and brown the meatballs, then remove to a plate.

Add the onions to the pan and gently cook for about five minutes, then add the mushrooms and continue to cook until they are soft and juicy.

Add the garlic, tomatoes, oregano, tomato purée, balsamic vinegar and wine and cook for a few minutes. Return the meatballs to the pan and cook for about 10 minutes, adding a splash of water if required to stop the mixture from becoming dry.

For the polenta, put the cold water and salt into a saucepan and stir in the polenta. Bring to a boil, stirring all the time, and then reduce to a simmer until the mixture thickens before adding the butter and cheese. The mixture should be similar in texture to mashed potatoes. (I put the cold water and polenta in together, as I find if I boil the water and then add the polenta it is far more difficult to get the right consistency.)

Serve the meatballs and sauce on top of the polenta, and garnish with parsley/basil.

Let food be
thy medicine and
medicine be thy food.
Hippocrates

MONIGA DEL GARDA,
BRESCIA

It was a moving day again today, Diary. A sense of sadness at leaving, but excitement too – I know that sounds like a contradiction, but I really do have those mixed feelings. We called in at the supermarket on the way out of town and stocked up for the next five days. I am finding this a good method to stay on top of my recipes and housekeeping, so that once we are parked up at a new campsite, we are self-sufficient in terms of not having to drive anywhere. We also topped up the tank with fuel, and we were ready to rumble.

Sally the sat-nav told us it was just over 100 miles to move up to Lake Garda, so a relatively quick journey today. Once on the autoroute we had a superb journey, 81 miles before we needed to turn off, and the roads were quiet. I turned on some tunes – I chose songs of the sixties, and I sang along to all of them.

Even though I was a child of the sixties, my parents were not hip in any way. I remember the records in Mum's collection were Victor Sylvester and Glen Miller-type things, certainly not The Beatles, Elvis, Dusty Springfield or the Mamas and the Papas. Anyway, Diary, it all felt very light, and the vibes were good as we sped along towards Garda.

As we were leaving the Lido di Jesolo area, I was reminded that back in the day it was a very on-trend resort. In the heyday of the 1970s, Lido was the place to go for some quality sun, sand and sex. That just made me smile – how do you quantify quality sex? Sun and sand yes, I get it, but for the sexy bit? Anyway, leaving the bucket and spade part of the trip behind us, we were destined for mountains and the lake, hopefully some sun, no sand and a good book!

We have been to Lake Garda a few times. The first was for John's 60th birthday, when I planned a surprise long weekend and we flew out and hired a little car. We stayed on a campsite in a mobile home and had a smashing time. We drove all around the lake in one day. Oh, that was a grand day out. Last year when we came to the Dolomites on a coach holiday, and we enjoyed a beautiful boat trip to Limone, one of the tiny coastal towns, so beautiful.

From afar I spotted the first mountain, rather hazy as the sun was fierce today. The landscape had changed too – now it was much greener, lots of vines and golden cornfields. As we drove along, we were overtaken by a Land Rover full of balloons and middle-aged men wearing coloured trilbies. They were hooting and waving, and I waved back – it was a joyful moment of connection. Strangers passing by, a smile and a wave, and then they were gone, where to and why left to my imagination.

We arrived, and it was so hot we could hardly bear it. We walked along the pebbly beach, but the heat sent us back to the campsite. I suggested a swim, but John declined, so I went to the pool to get my daily swim under my belt. Alas, the pool was heaving, every sun lounger either occupied by a human or a towel. I found a plastic chair and dumped my things to approach the pool. Every new pool must be appraised by me, not for health-and-safety reasons, well actually it is kind of for that, as I'm working out how to get into the pool as quickly

John pointed out tall spires, or are they towers? They reminded me of pencils, standing slim and straight and, along with the cypress trees that are abundant once again, it made for a striking landscape. John loves mountains, and he is not a sun and sand chap, and the least said about that the better, wink, wink! I know he's looking forward to this part of the trip, along with our next stop which is Switzerland. I mentally reset my intentions again, to try to be kinder!

and unobtrusively as possible. Not being as svelte as I once was, I like to make a discreet entry into the water. I normally check out where the steps are, the depth and so on, before I decide how to approach the situation. At this campsite there are lovely Roman steps, that in theory I should be able to step down gracefully and glide into the water. No, Diary, it was impossible to do this, as five teenage Italian girls sat in their bikinis on the steps.

I waited 10 minutes thinking they would go and swim, but not a chance, they were chatting and posing right under the nose of the lifeguard, who made no attempt to move them on to allow an elderly lady like me the opportunity of entering the pool. I went to the other side and, with no grace, managed to lower myself to a sitting position, but not without rolling backwards and hitting the back of my head on the ground! I collected myself and slithered into the water. What a relief, the water was cool, fresh and quite wonderful.

Thus, refreshed, and with the heat of the sun abating a little, I made our dinner. It is pasta again. Oh dear John, all I can say is, when in Rome (well in Garda), do as the Italians do. It is a ragù with pappardelle pasta. Pappardelle is long, like spaghetti, but made in thick strips. We ate, watching the lake starting to twinkle with the lights from the towns on the coastline. We have a good view from our van. It is beautiful, set in an old olive grove, perfect really.

After eating dinner, we wandered down to the lakeside – cool now and lovely. A portly gentleman strode down to the water purposefully, stripped off to his boxers and was in the lake in a flash. There were children with fishing nets trying their luck, and John tried to skim a few pebbles. We saw a family of ducks and ducklings, teenage ducklings I guess as they were getting large and were paddling about on the scrounge for supper. We could hear music too, well if you can call it that, as karaoke was blaring out from the busy and bright restaurant! Everything was all good tonight, and I had that feeling of wellbeing after a good day with no issues or niggles.

Goodnight diary, sleep well!

– Day 18 Recipe –
RAGÙ WITH PAPPARDELLE

In Italian cuisine, ragù is a meat-based sauce that is served with pasta. For the recipe I have used venison mince and pappardelle pasta, but any mince and pasta will work well. This version of ragù is dark, rich and glossy and is finished with a few spoonfuls of pasta water. Italians like to mix the cooked pasta into the ragù and then serve with some parmesan cheese on the top.

Ingredients (serves 2)

- 2 tablespoons olive oil
- 1 onion, finely chopped
- 500g venison mince (or beef)
- 1 tablespoon tomato purée
- 3 garlic cloves, crushed
- 1 tablespoon dried thyme
- 100ml beef stock
- 2 tablespoons balsamic vinegar
- 200ml red wine
- 400ml carton of passata
- Salt and pepper
- 8 dried coils of pappardelle pasta
- 2 tablespoons table salt
- Parmesan cheese

Method

In a large frying pan, heat the oil and soften the onion for about five minutes. Add the minced venison, and brown well. Add the tomato purée, garlic and thyme, and mix well.

Add the balsamic vinegar and the stock. Bring to the boil, then turn the heat down and simmer until the liquid has reduced by half.

Add the wine and passata. Bubble to a boil, and then reduce to a simmer until the ragù is quite thick and most of the liquid has reduced.

While the ragu is simmering, bring a large pan of water to a boil and add two tablespoons of table salt. Once boiling, add the pasta to the pan and cook for about 12 minutes or until the pasta is al dente.

Add a few tablespoons of pasta water to the ragù and stir it in. Drain the pasta before adding it to the ragù, mixing well to ensure the pasta is coated in the sauce.

Serve with a sprinkle of parmesan.

Life is a combination of magic and pasta.

Federico Fellini

– Day 19 –

MONIGA DEL GARDA,
BRESCIA

What a flipping day, Diary! It's been good in parts but with some frustrations. The day started well – I was up with the larks once again and the weather was nice and fresh, not too hot. We had made plans to get off the site to visit another resort along the coast. There are very limited ferries from this town, only a couple a day, so we decided to travel by bus. Remember we are now well versed in the intricacies of Italian buses, so off we went, armed with a timetable and optimistic for a good day ahead.

The walk from our campsite to the town is only about a kilometre, but it's all uphill. By the time we set off, the sun was starting to warm things up and I was soon huffing and blowing like a broken winded horse. John, older but much fitter than I, strode on giving me tips: 'Don't look up, look at the ground, you will soon be at the top.' I stopped now and then to catch my breath and try to stay in the moment, looking at the hedgerows, different grasses, some fast-fading

we thought – and they had a rack of swimming costumes by the door. I took a look and they had my size, but for 69 euros, absolutely not! I pay £20 maximum back home.

The goose-chase begins again diary. Following the directions given, and accompanied by Google Maps, we did eventually find a bus stop; however, there weren't any buses! We waited, and I kept asking Google, which told us to keep walking, and we found ourselves back in the square by the lingerie shop where we started off. We were both running with sweat and a bit brassed-off by now. We gave up. Defeated, we went into a café for a drink to revive us.

Walking down the hill back to the campsite was much easier, but our hearts were a bit heavy. We decided to go and investigate the ferries again. We found a café that sold tickets for the ferry and had a bite of lunch. The waitress took our order of a hot dog and a cheese toastie, and confirmed that

honeysuckle, and some pretty wild flowers. 'That's right', John commented, 'smell the roses'. I looked around for roses, but there were none – 'It's just an expression!' said John.

As we reached the top of the hill there were vines, rows and rows stretching out far away, the tiny grapes just starting to show themselves. What better reminder than this that we are in scalding-hot Italy.

We went on the search for bus tickets, but that was a non-starter. After being directed to various shops we were told in Italian that you buy them on the bus. OK, we think, next question I ask is: 'Where is the bus stop?' After some scratching of heads, eventually some hand and arm movements indicated to us where to go. We thought we were nearly sorted, not long now. On a different note, the shop we were in to try to buy bus tickets also sold lingerie – a bit odd

buses are difficult here and the ferries do run, but not very often. She reels off the times and we say we will think it over.

With today's travel plans abandoned, we go back to the motorhome and, in an effort to avoid the midday sun, we dropped the bed down from the roof and had a siesta. We snoozed for about an hour and then decided to go down to the pool. Remembering how packed the pool was yesterday we had low expectations; however, we were in luck. We found sunbeds. We artfully arranged our towels to proclaim them as engaged, and entered the water. This time I made full use of the Roman steps – no crashing about on the paving flags today!

After about 10 minutes we were back on the sunbeds. I noticed – well it would have been hard not to – the girls from yesterday were next to us along with a couple of boyfriends. There were lots of entwined bodies, and hands stroking bums, the romance quite palpable even from my sunbed. I can't help but look, recalling the time 40-odd years ago when that was me, and not an Italian lover but a Greek one. I smile and feel pleased that the world still turns in the same direction as it always has, love first!

In and out of the pool we went, to cool off. It was very nice, and washed away the morning's frustrations. Some of the entertainment team turned up whilst I was on my sunbed (with my dress on my head acting as a shield from the sun!). Music blaring, they started dancing, and quite a few people knew the steps and the words and joined them. It was quite a

spectacle, still the youngsters in the throes of passion on one side of me, and dancing Italian girls on the other. John wasn't sure which way to look!

Eventually, when the sun had lost some of its heat, we ventured back to the motorhome. John did some of the housekeeping tasks – filling and emptying water and so on –

while I made tonight's meal, Milanaise chicken with pizzaiola sauce and a side of Milanaise risotto. Possibly a little bit more coordination needed for this recipe, but the process is quick enough, and the risotto – made with saffron, which ounce for ounce is more expensive than gold – is bright summer yellow. A real feast for the eyes.

Diary, by now you know about John's dietary requirements. I won't go on, but I could tell he was not fond of that rice. No amount of me talking to him about the saffron and the parmesan could tempt him, and after a few mouthfuls he left it. I said nothing, as I'm learning about old dogs and new tricks.

The evening is cooler now, and not hazy as it was yesterday. We can see all the way across the lake, and we are determined to try again tomorrow to get away from our little patch of Garda. We will attempt the ferry again and this time we won't be defeated.

On that note Diary, I wish you goodnight!

– Day 19 Recipe –

CHICKEN MILANAISE WITH PIZZAIOLA SAUCE AND RISOTTO MILANAISE

The breaded and pan-fried chicken in this recipe originated in Milan and the sauce from Naples. The sauce can be served with fish too, or stirred through pasta. I recommend that you prepare the chicken first and keep it in the fridge until ready to pan fry it. For ease, I used breadcrumbs bought from the supermarket, but you could grate your own. The sauce in its simplest form is just oil, garlic, tomatoes, oregano and salt, but I like to add the extras to make it even more representative of pizza!

The risotto hails from Milan too, and is arguably the most popular risotto in Italy. The sunshine yellow colour comes from the pinch of saffron used in the recipe. Saffron is the most expensive spice there is, but the earthy taste and beautiful colour is exquisite. You could substitute turmeric at a pinch, excuse the pun!

Ingredients (serves 2)

Risotto Milanaise
- 1 tablespoon butter
- 1 onion, diced
- 90g *(half a cup)* risotto rice
- A good pinch of saffron
- 300ml hot stock
- 50ml white wine, vermouth, or Aperol
- Salt and pepper
- Handful of parmesan cheese

Chicken Milanaise
- 2 chicken breasts
- 4 tablespoons flour
- Salt and pepper
- Half teaspoon chilli flakes
- 1 beaten egg
- 8 tablespoons breadcrumbs
- Several tablespoons oil

Pizzaiola sauce
- 2 tablespoons extra-virgin olive oil
- 3 cloves of garlic, crushed
- 1 tablespoon tomato purée
- Handful of cherry tomatoes
- 1 tablespoon dried oregano
- 2 tablespoons black olives, sliced
- 1 tablespoon capers
- Splash of Worcestershire sauce
- Splash of red wine
- Water to loosen
- Salt and pepper

Method

Risotto

Melt the butter in a frying pan and then add the onion and cook on a gentle heat until soft. Add the rice and cook for a few minutes, stirring all the time.

Add the saffron to the stock. Add a cupful of the stock to the pan and sizzle that down until it is absorbed. Continue to add the stock, one cupful at a time – once each cupful of stock is absorbed, add the next. It is important to stir most of the time, so that the rice becomes creamy in consistency.

When nearly all the stock is absorbed, add the alcohol and salt and pepper to taste. When the rice is tender, and the liquid is all absorbed, stir in most of the cheese, leaving some to scatter on the top. Cover with foil to keep warm, while you make the chicken and sauce.

Chicken

Using a sharp knife, carefully slice each chicken breast horizontally to give you four thin escalopes.

Prepare two plates and one bowl. Pour the flour onto a plate and season it with salt, pepper and chilli flakes. Spread the breadcrumbs on a second plate and put the beaten egg into a bowl. Dip each escalope into the flour, and then dip into the beaten egg. Coat each escalope in breadcrumbs, pressing them down firmly with your fingers.

Heat the oil in the frying pan and then shallow-fry the chicken on each side for five minutes, approximately 10 minutes in total. Turn frequently to ensure the breadcrumbs are golden, not burnt! Add more oil if required, as the breadcrumbs tend to absorb it.

When the chicken is cooked, keep warm in foil while you make the sauce.

Sauce

Warm the oil in a frying pan and gently cook the garlic for a minute. Add the tomato purée, fresh tomatoes, oregano, olives, capers, Worcestershire sauce and salt and pepper.

Loosen with a little water and the wine, adjusting the consistency as you wish.

There is no love sincerer than the love of food.

George Bernard Shaw

– *Day 20* –

MONIGA DEL GARDA,
BRESCIA

Diary, I am tucked up in bed now at the end of another day, day 20 in fact, tempus fugit! I am nursing a few cuts and bruises; a deep graze on my left foot, a chunk out of my left elbow, a twinge in my left knee and a big lump out of my dignity. Let me tell you what happened.

It was just about an hour or so ago and I was happily setting up the dining table for tonight's dinner. I was stepping out of the motorhome and onto a small stepping stool (the motorhome is a bit high off the ground because it is on ramps to level it, so we need an extra step). Anyway, I was just coming out with a glass of prosecco in one hand and some cutlery in the other, the step gave way and I crashed to the ground.

I am always a bit over-dramatic when this type of thing happens, and I was howling and shouting whilst at the same moment trying to work out if I had badly hurt myself and needed medical attention. An Italian lady came running over, as did a woman from Hungary, both speaking in their native languages. John, who had been topping up the screenwash, came to the scene of the accident more slowly, saying in his mother tongue: 'What the bloody hell have you done now?'

They helped me up from the dusty ground, and the ladies retreated to their mobile homes. John helped me to hobble to a seat and dusted me down. We cleaned up my cuts and grazes and we restored order. I was keen to get dinner on the table, as I needed to photograph it whilst there was good daylight. I plated it up, did the photoshoot and we settled down to eat. 'OUCH!', I had leaned on my injured elbow, and it was excruciating. John still had the camera in his hand, and I could hardly believe it when I was going through the photos just now, and he had taken a picture of my agony!

Back to this morning... After yesterday's attempt at getting out of town, I was more determined than ever to escape over the water and visit Sermione, arguably one of the prettiest and most visited places on Lake Garda. We established there

whole way, with nothing but the back of someone's chair to steady ourselves. It was a half-hour trip, so not the most comfortable way to travel.

It was worth it though when we disembarked at Sermione. It was very pretty, with a medieval castle overlooking the town square and the many small and quaint narrow streets. It was busy, very busy, all us tourists milling about like ants. I lost count of the number of gelateria selling copious mounds of ice

was a ferry over at lunchtime and one back around 4.30: after spending a morning catching up with a few housekeeping jobs and a bit of correspondence, we set off to get the ferry. We bought the tickets and waited on the jetty. A few more people joined us, some with bikes, and we saw the small ferry approaching. When it was close enough to see clearly, we realised it was packed. Anyway, we were squeezed on board like sardines in a can, an oily can at that, and we stood the

cream. I tried to sneak a photo, but those ice-cream vendors are wise to every click, and I got wagging fingers back at me, effectively telling me no!

We were hungry for lunch but, as is often the case with John and I, we weren't sure where to go. We didn't want anything too swish, worried about the cost to our purse, so we roamed the back streets and somehow found a greasy spoon, or the

Italian equivalent. I don't know why, but we sat down and ate there. There was nothing wrong with the food, but the ambience was a bit lacking! We wandered around marvelling at the gorgeous shops and the nooks and crannies. I found a cool set of steps to rest for a minute – cool in the real sense of the word, as the stone steps were shaded from the sun. A moment of sanctuary.

We wandered again, and found a water fountain. We washed our hands to cool us down a bit and then sheltered from the heat on a bench in the shade. We people-watched for a bit and saw a man and two young boys walking towards us, each with the biggest ice-cream cone I think I have ever seen. Unusually for me, I initiate a conversation with a comment about the cones. They are British, from Liverpool. What a lovely family.

We chat for ages while they try to eat the dripping cones. They had ridden hired bikes from a nearby campsite, which we had worked on occasionally in the past. We compared notes and he asked us for tips about similar campsites that might be good for the boys. We ended up discussing bicycle helmets, of all things. The dad, who works in car crashes (insurance), would always wear a helmet even for a short trip. He tells us how his helmet might have saved him yesterday when the brakes on his Italian hired bike were back to front, he squeezed what he thought was the back brake but it was the front, and he went over the top. He and I are both now wearing injuries for the world to see. The boys washed their sticky hands in the fountain, and we bid them farewell, another set of people we meet fleetingly, leaving only their impression on my memory.

We queued for the ferry in good time, as we wanted a seat going back. We chatted in line to a couple from the UK who are touring, like us, in a motorhome. This is always very helpful as you learn about places and things to see, as well as things maybe to avoid. My seat going back was on the sunny side, so I was still hot and had a German toddler almost sitting on my shoulders, with the child's mum chattering every second of the trip. I was irritated by this. At my feet

brought a small wooden crate with a bag of crisps, nuts, olives, pickles, very cute indeed and excellent value. Lovely drinks and treats, and all for 10 euros.

Once back at the site, I went for my swim. Hallelujah, I have found the right window for my swim – only nine of us were in the pool, all grey-haired, and one lady must have been as old as Methuselah. Not a bathing beauty or a squirming lothario

was a huge dog, which looked placid enough, even though it was wearing a soft muzzle. I felt a bit sorry for the dog, as the muzzle makes you think it's a dangerous dog, but it's probably for its own safety. Still, I was careful when I moved my feet.

Diary, this day seems long. I will cut to the chase then. Once off the boat we went immediately to buy cold drinks – beer for John, water and lemon soda for me. I noticed before that in Italy you get snacks for free with drinks. In this café they

to be seen! I did, however, see one chap – a grey-haired one – stroking his wife's arms in a very seductive way! It was very nice to see – love will endure!

I made our dinner, a carbonara, and the last pasta dish of the trip – John is relieved! After my tumble out of the motorhome, I drink some more prosecco for medicinal purposes and here I am. It's been a lovely day overall, memorable!

Until tomorrow, good night!

– Day 20 Recipe –
BREAKFAST CARBONARA

Carbonara is one of the most popular pasta dishes around, certainly it is one of my favourites. I love a creamy sauce, but authentic carbonara does not contain cream, just egg yolks mixed with some starchy pasta water to make the silky sauce. In this campsite-friendly version, I have removed the eggs and added a tub of mascarpone. The addition of some finely chopped sausages, cherry tomatoes, and finely-sliced mushrooms to the standard lardons or bacon make this a hearty meal, lovely as breakfast, lunch or dinner!

Ingredients (serves 2)

- 6 coils tagliatelle
- 1 tablespoon salt
- 2 tablespoons oil
- 2 rashers smoked streaky bacon, or small pack of smoked lardons
- 2 pork sausages, sliced
- 4 cloves garlic, crushed
- 8 mushrooms, finely sliced
- Handful cherry tomatoes, halved
- 1 teaspoon smoked paprika
- Salt and pepper
- 200ml mascarpone *(or cream)*
- A piece of parmesan or cheddar cheese *(about size of two matchboxes)*, grated

Method

Fill a large pan with water, add one tablespoon of salt and bring to a boil. Add the tagliatelle and cook according to the pack instructions or until 'al dente', which is soft but still with a little resistance when you bite it.

Meanwhile, dice the bacon and slice the sausages. Heat the oil in a frying pan and add the sausage chunks. Cook for 10 minutes, add the bacon and cook for a couple more minutes.

Add the mushrooms, garlic and tomatoes to the pan, mix well and cook until the mushrooms have wilted and are soft. This takes a few minutes.

Season with salt and pepper and add the smoked paprika.

Mix in the mascarpone and then add the grated cheese and a couple of tablespoons of pasta water to the pan.

Drain, but don't rinse, the tagliatelle and reserve a little cooking water. Add the drained pasta to the sauce and stir well, loosening with a little of the reserved pasta water if needed.

Spaghetti is eaten most successfully if you inhale it like a vacuum cleaner.

Sophia Loren

What I think of when I think of Switzerland is royalty...

Don't misunderstand me, I don't mean in the 'kings and queens' sense – she has been a republic since 1848.

I mean as a country she feels regal, top of the class in the mountains department, clean, orderly and slightly intimidating. She is dramatic, serene and elegant.

She commands respect!

I have visited Switzerland several times. When we worked for the holiday company, we had one campsite there. We always went at the start and the end of the season to winterise and then reopen the mobile homes. The campsite was at Interlaken on the banks of Lake Thun, such a great location.

My husband John is mountain mad; he was a climber in his younger days, so this location was manna from heaven for him. We could see the Jungfrau from the campsite at Interlacken (when it was a clear sky at least, which surprisingly it mostly was). On one occasion we were there on his birthday. His birthday treat was a ride on the train right to the top of the Jungfrau. At the café at the top, it was gloriously warm and sunny, and we had a massive slice of apple strudel and cream, wrong country for it of course, as strudel belongs in Austria but we devoured it all the same.

When I think of Swiss food I think of cheese and chocolate, both of which are rumoured to give you nightmares! Alpine food, whether it be Swiss, French or Austrian shares many similarities. It does involve lots of cheese, especially in France and Switzerland. Fondue, tartiflette and raclette are all popular. Potatoes feature in many dishes too – climbing mountains and walking in the Alps take up lots of energy so you need to stock up on filling foods.

The alpine landscape is totally stunning in every direction – everywhere you look there is spectacular scenery. Mountains of course, grassy alps, cows with their clanking bells, icy cold streams, gushing waterfalls, lakes and then of course the cute picture postcard villages with the white spiky spires of the churches and the wooden chalets all decked out with the window boxes full of colour.

Switzerland has four national languages but German is the most commonly spoken language in Switzerland. As hard as I try, and believe me I try everywhere I go to get a grip of the basics in a language, I cannot get into German. So, in the supermarkets and shops I am totally reliant on what I can recognise on the shelves. So far, I have not come a cropper and bought something strange by mistake but of course there is a first time for everything. Perhaps on this trip we will get an opportunity to have a meal in a restaurant, what might be on the menu? Cheese of course or chocolate, so no complaints from me!

On this trip it is yet again a flying visit, not literally of course, we are still in the motorhome but at least we are heading for a completely new campsite. A new area for us which I am thrilled about. It will be brilliant to see this spectacular country from a new perspective rather than working. This time we are on holiday!

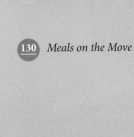

– Day 21 –

LEUKERBAD,
VALAIS

After 12 days in Italy, we packed up and headed north this morning. We had a blast, four regions that were all very different. I wouldn't want to choose a favourite, they all offered up some wonderful sights and experiences. If I was really pushed, I think I would plump for Venice. I fell in love with the city.

Anyway Diary, onwards and upwards. Literally upwards, as we headed north out of Italy via Milan, then passing by Lake Maggiore. We only got a very quick glimpse, between tunnels, but it looked fantastic, and I bet it is a quieter place than Garda to visit. I shall put it on my list of places to visit on my next trip to Italy.

I had, as is quite normal for me, forgotten to eat breakfast. We found ourselves in a traffic jam due to a three-car collision on the autoroute towards Milan.

As the traffic was at a standstill, I popped into the fridge and retrieved a portion of last night's dinner. Breakfast carbonara, totally suitable for breakfast today! Now, my cousin Janet will not eat anything cold that was once hot, but I always do – the flavours intensify and for me it tastes even more delicious. I think it was way back when I lived in Greece that I got used to eating food that was not red hot. Of course, you do need to watch the food-hygiene element, as otherwise you could get a nasty dose of the trots! The funny thing was that when I sat down in the passenger seat to eat, I noticed that the Tupperware had a printed label on it, a relic from some food festival I must have worked at, and the label said... Swiss Roll. And here I was on my way to Switzerland. I even took a photograph to prove it!

We stopped at a service station for a lunch break. We are self-sufficient being in the motorhome and can knock up a sandwich in minutes. However, I had a craving for some sweets, so I went to buy a selection – a Mars bar, a Lion bar, two packets of Haribo and a can of my now favourite soft drink, lemon soda. Sugar rush over, we continued on our way.

The journey today was a long one, 200 miles, but took quite a few hours more than we expected. First there was the traffic jam and then, even though the roads after Milan were quiet, they were a bit winding, with tunnels and hairpin bends, but beautiful nonetheless.

My mind wandered to languages as we drove along. My dad, as I have said before, spent more than five years in Italy during the war. He liked to think he was a linguist, and when we

went on our first trip abroad when I was 13, to Ibiza, I was mortified when he tried to speak to the waiters in Italian. He told me it was pretty much the same as Spanish! Of course, they couldn't understand a single word he said to them. As an adult, my mum, who has spent lots of time in Spain and thinks she can speak a bit of the lingo, was once visiting us in our holiday home in France (rural France at that, where most folks have never been further away than the nearest big city). Someone knocked at the door and when I opened it the man explained in French that he was our local farmer, and he grazes his cattle on our portion of field up the lane. Mum, who had been decorating one of the rooms, came to the door and pulled him indoors to admire her handiwork, saying 'mucho trabajo, mucho trabajo' which translated means 'much work, much work', but she was speaking Spanish to a French farmer! At least French, Italian and Spanish are all romance languages, so with that common denominator there have to be some similarities.

I had two failed interactions today with the Italian toll booths. I put in my ticket followed by my credit card, but nothing happened. Just as I was starting to feel a bit panicky, an invoice spat out and the barrier went up and off we sped. I read the invoices, which said I must pay online within 15 days – something else to battle with! It's all a learning curve, that much is certain.

We leave Italy, announced as always by my mobile phone before we see any border signs. I thought we needed to buy a vignette. A vignette is to cover Swiss road taxes. We stop at a deserted ticket office. I see a trucker from Lithuania putting a card in a slot. I copied him, and I honestly thought the machine was eating my card, as the grinding noises were horrific. It spat my card back out. Then I read the instructions, and it was asking me to insert an identity card. Oops, we don't have them do we! I picked up a leaflet, which

said download an app. I did, but it kept asking me to scan my T1 and T2 documents. I was just about to give up all hope, when I noticed uniformed border guards arrive at the office, who must have been on a lunch break. I sauntered over and shouted: 'Hello'. No response, so I tried again, and with obvious reluctance one of the men looked at me. I said: 'Vignette?' He replied in very cold tones: 'You don't need a vignette if you don't use the autoroute, go.' Feeling chastened, as this was a mountain pass and clearly not an autoroute, I went back to the motorhome, and we left. 'Bloody tourists!', I'm sure he probably said to his colleagues.

The terrain is all you would expect in Switzerland: snowcapped mountains, blue skies interspersed with ominous grey clouds, alps with cattle jangling their bells, birds of prey soaring on thermals, hairpin bends and a human roller-coaster ride through the Simplon Pass. We both felt fantastic, and somehow we could tell the air was fresher and cleaner, and we were both keen to find our campsite and settle for two nights.

It was easy enough, no issues with navigating with the helpful Sally the sat-nav in front of us. We settled on the small but perfectly formed campsite, and had a relaxing evening. The recipe for today was a simple one – potato rosti with fried eggs, a near relation of egg and chips. John is very happy to be reintroduced to spuds, and I cooked up a pan of mushrooms, lardons and sausages to eat alongside it. All very nice, and

John and I shared a bottle of wine. I took a call from my brother from another mother, Mark, who designed this book, to chat through some ideas, and then I listened to the Bee Gees, a bit random I know, but Spotify told me to!

That's day 21 in the bag, Diary, and it's time to explore Switzerland tomorrow.

Guten tag!

– Day 21 Recipe –
POTATO ROSTI WITH FRIED EGGS

This is a great dish to have for brunch. Potato rosti is a genuine Swiss classic and very moreish. Hash browns are a close relation, but this is the real deal!

Ingredients (serves 2)

- 2 large baking-sized potatoes, grated *(unpeeled)*
- 1 beaten egg
- 2 tablespoons plain flour
- Salt and pepper
- Half a small onion, finely grated
- 3 tablespoons oil
- 2 eggs *(for frying)*

Method

Squeeze out as much excess water as possible from the grated potatoes by wrapping them in a clean tea towel.

Mix the grated potato with the onion, flour, salt and pepper and the beaten egg.

Heat the oil in a frying pan. Form the mixture into small patties, or one large rosti.

Place the rostis into the hot pan, press them down with the back of a spoon or spatula, and cook for five minutes or so on each side until golden brown and very crisp.

Serve with a fried egg on the top!

What I say is this, if a man really likes potatoes, he must be a decent sort of fellow.

AA Milne

– Day 22 –

LEUKERBAD,
VALAIS

It was the summer solstice today, Diary – the longest day of the year and the official start of summer, the day when the sun seems to stand still. I was thinking about it, about Stonehenge and all the rituals and ceremonies that have taken place there over the centuries, and wondering how it got built and why. All the sweet mysteries of life surround such things.

Here we are still in Switzerland, and not a druid to be seen, no indication of anything mystical occurring at all. I am a bit that

take the motorhome for a trip up a mountain. Although the location of this campsite is very pleasant, you do need transport to get up those mountains. We didn't want to go far, as I was keen to have some time on the site resting and relaxing, reading and writing. Off we went and found ourselves climbing up from Sierre, a valley town, on a very scenic route past lots of vineyards and wineries and up towards Crans-Montana. John tells me this is a popular skiing place often featured on *Ski Sunday* on the television. We went

way inclined these days, Diary – you may have noticed me edging slightly towards a more spiritual way of thinking. I like to try as hard as possible to remain in the moment, though I fail at least once most days, but that must be an improvement on never being in the moment and my brain always running like the clappers, thinking about the future.

So here we are, day 22 over and out. There was no swimming today or yesterday, as we have no pool, no sea, no lake, not even a stream to paddle in. This morning we decided to

up and up, around and around, hairpin bends and sheer drops! We got to the top and parked up.

We took a short stroll towards the village. It was midday and the church bells started to toll, John asked if it was Sunday! No, I said: 'It's Wednesday.' The village was not as chocolate-box perfect as you might find elsewhere, but it had its own charm, and I think it was quite old. There were alpine-style houses of course, with window boxes of geraniums, but also very old, wooden barns, one for every house. We speculated on what they stored in them – not wood for the fires, as that was all piled up at the sides of the houses under shelters. Probably hay for wintering the cattle.

The village was deserted except for a family of four eating lunch on their patio, and a little girl on a skateboard who chirped: 'Bonjour monsieur, madame.' Ha, ha, thought I, they speak French up here in the mountains, good! We returned to the motorhome and retraced our journey back down to the

same week). I took a sneaky photograph and pinged it over to him. Terry agreed with me that he was a doppelganger and also said that his Instagram account had been hacked, so there was someone impersonating him on social media, as well as here on the campsite!

Chatting with Terry made me think back to my days on *Bake Off*. It was almost five years ago now, and there have been a lot of changes for me since then. It was a massive learning

valley. We needed to fill up with fuel and buy a few bits from the Co-Op (of all places!), and then we returned to the site.

We just chilled out this afternoon and I really enjoyed it. I did some people-watching from afar and noticed that the guy on the pitch next door is a dead-ringer for my friend Terry (who was on the *Bake Off* with me, and we got eliminated on the

curve, getting on that show. I had the time of my life, although it wasn't all a bed of roses, with lots of ups and downs, but overall it was an amazing experience.

I learned so many things, not just how to bake, but how to trust my instincts, and how to watch for and take up opportunities, even when you think there are none. The opportunities are there, you just need to look for them and catch and cage them while you can.

I often wonder where I would be now if those opportunities had come calling say 20 years ago, when I was younger and still trying to carve out a career. I always wanted to work with food, or in entertainment, but it didn't happen back then. It seems now in the years when most of my friends are looking forward to retirement,

I am just getting started with my cooking, baking, and entertaining (well, I hope I entertain and don't send folks into a coma!).

Enough of all this introspection, back to the present. For dinner today I made raclette. Raclette is a cheese commonly found in French and Swiss alpine areas, but it is also the term for a cooking gadget. I left my electric raclette at home as I wanted to keep things simple, so it was an improvisation on my gas BBQ. Simple and delicious. John was happy once more, as it is fundamentally meat and two veg, back in his comfort zone once again.

Time tomorrow to move on again, Diary, back into France. The countdown is on now to the end of our trip together. Let's make the most of it and squeeze everything we can out of every day. It's thundering outside again so it's definitely time for bed. À bientôt!

– Day 22 Recipe –
RACLETTE

Raclette is a type of cheese, commonly found in the alpine areas of France and Switzerland. It is also a cooking utensil – typically, a small tabletop grill with two functions: the top to griddle meat and vegetables, and underneath you melt the raclette cheese in small pans. When you use this sort of gadget, raclette is a communal meal, where each person cooks their own selection of food and melts their own cheese too, so it's lots of fun.

If you don't have a raclette grill, then it is less of a communal experience, but tastes just the same and is easy. All you need is a stove-top griddle pan and a small frying pan to melt the cheese.

The selection of meats is entirely your choice, but everything needs to be sliced into small strips or chunks. The same with vegetables: strips of peppers, onions, mushrooms, baby corn, asparagus tips and cherry tomatoes all work well. I used thin steak and chicken goujons, but sliced pork, gammon, sausage, or even fish would be perfect.

If you can't find raclette cheese, any melting cheese (like Emmental, gruyère or cheddar) will work.

Ingredients (serves 2)

- 1 tablespoon oil
- Seasoning spices/paprika/peri peri/chilli flakes according to your preference
- Salt and pepper
- Strips of beef steak and chicken (*see note above about alternatives*)
- Strips of vegetables (*see above*)
- A matchbox-sized chunk of cheese per person, preferably raclette
- A handful of cooked baby/new potatoes per person

Method

Rub the meat strips and vegetables in a little oil and sprinkle with your choice of seasoning spices and salt and pepper.

Heat the raclette grill or your griddle pan, and cook the meat and vegetables first. For the meat, cook for about five minutes per side, ensuring that it is cooked to your liking, but the times will vary depending on the thickness of the meat. Steak strips cook very fast, just a matter of a few minutes to medium-rare. The vegetables can be cooked alongside the meat.

Melt the cheese either under the raclette grill or on the stove top in a small pan.

Serve the meat and vegetables with the potatoes on the side. Pour the melted cheese over the potatoes.

Many's the long night I've dreamed of cheese — toasted mostly.

Robert Louis Stevenson

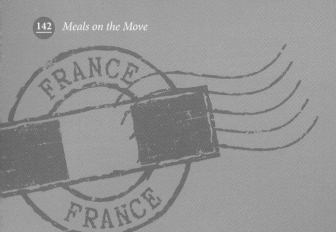

Returning to France...

When I thought of Alsace, Lorraine, and the north-east of France I expected low-lying land and vast open spaces – I did not imagine the mountains, the valleys and the undulating landscape.

I didn't expect the picture-postcard villages or the hilltop castles. What a glorious place, I am so happy to have finally made its acquaintance! I must come back for a visit soon so I can stop and linger longer in its towns, forests, villages and valleys.

À bientôt eastern France!

As human beings, we build up expectations about both people and places. It is often folly to do so, as often those expectations are not met. However, sometimes our expectations are low, for whatever reason, and what a joy it is when reality blows those expectations out of the water. Interesting phrase that, I must look up where it comes from! When I planned this trip, I had never spent any real time in the areas we were going to stay in eastern France, so I was not sure what to expect. What would the landscape be like? What sort of towns and villages would we see? I had no idea, but was so pleasantly surprised.

After leaving the wondrous and breathtaking Switzerland behind us, I was worried that the landscape would become bland and possibly even boring (although I always think if you have an inquisitive mind, you can never be bored). The landscape had already calmed down from those rugged snowcapped mountains to more rolling valleys and lush and verdant green fields in the valley bottoms, but as soon as we hit France I was struck by how attractive it was. The houses around Colmar, which was our first port of call, are old, timber framed, but for the most part painted between the frames in shades of red and burnt orange. We only spent two nights in that area, but it felt like coming home, as I understood the tempo of the area and I felt in tune with everything.

We moved on about 60 miles up the country to Alsace, where Germany is so close that many of the street names are very Germanic. The Vosges mountains sit on the French side of the border and are quite low and dark-looking. We were treated to those fairytale castles atop hills in the far distance, and the lovely church spires, reminding me of scenes from Christmas cards – without the snow of course, so some imagination was needed, but I have an abundance of that. The air looked and felt fresher, although it was not cold, as the sun was still high in the sky and illuminated everything so beautifully.

As we moved further up and into north-eastern France, towards the Belgian border, the landscape changed again. It was still pretty, but much flatter, and the churches were built in a completely different style here. The towns looked like places where ordinary everyday folk would have been, and still are, living for generations, making a living from the land and small industries here and there.

The final leg of our journey took us across the top of the country and back from whence we started this trip 30 days before, close to Calais. This region was still rather flat, and perhaps less interesting to look at, but there, like everywhere, if you scratch the surface, fascinating things are just waiting to be discovered. The farming and heavy industry keeps the cogs of a country turning – it must take place for us to survive, and that gives the landscape a beauty of its very own. Not that this area was ugly in any way, but it wasn't the picture-postcard scenery that we have become used to on our trip. I appreciated it more for that, and somehow I felt at ease and comfortable with this part of France and the other eastern areas I have seen for the first time in my life. I will return soon; I would like to linger for longer in these chilled-out places. These towns and villages, hills and valleys must hold secrets, and they are steeped in so much history.

In my introduction to France, I started with a few lines from a poem: 'How much do I love thee, let me count the ways.' Having spent a week exploring this new area of the country, I can conclude that I love eastern France very much indeed.

– Day 23 –

COLMAR,
HAUT-RHIN

We moved campsite again today, Diary, back into France. The journey from Switzerland into France was the easiest yet, good roads that were easy to navigate, so Sally sat-nav could have taken the day off. And no tolls at all, meaning no extra expenses and no stressing out with toll booths that don't say 'yes'. That reminds me, Diary, I did go online and pay those Italian invoices. After about three attempts where the computer said 'no', I finally cracked it, so I don't have to worry about nasty letters and fines from the Italian tax man.

cover perhaps? The author, Joanna Spry, wrote the book towards the end of the 1880s, so it wasn't new even when I was a girl. I Googled the story as we drove, and decided to get a copy for my granddaughter, Silke. She is nearly seven now and can read, and with her long, blonde hair, she also reminds me of Heidi.

Driving along is good for thinking and musing – well, as a passenger at any rate. The next thing that occurs to me is how I wished I had hung onto my books from childhood, not just

The journey through Switzerland was very interesting. You may think it is all mountains and alpine villages, but the landscape was ever-changing: rugged mountains, some snowcapped, miles upon miles of vineyards, fruit orchards, quarries, hilltop castles, flat and wide valley bottoms with tinkling streams and the cows joining in with their cowbells. It was beautiful! We drove past Lac Léman, which is massive and almost looked like it was the sea, but I knew it couldn't be, with Switzerland being landlocked. The weather was quite hazy which somehow added to the vista.

As we sped along, I was thinking of the book, *Heidi*. I remember reading a copy as a child in the sixties. I imagined a lovely fresh-faced girl with long blonde plaits in traditional costume. Maybe that was how she was depicted on the book

Heidi but I had a children's cookery book, hardbacked and bigger than A4. How I loved looking through that book, and having a go at some of the recipes. It's out of print now, but I have seen it on eBay, so I must try to buy a copy. I was also thinking about my collection of dolls in country costumes. It was a fad back then to collect them. Nobody I knew travelled abroad, so how I came by them I have no idea. They were about the size of Barbie dolls: I had a Native American, a Dutch girl, a Spanish flamenco dancer, one from Denmark and a few others. They were all the same build, and all pretty dolls, except the Welsh girl, who was shorter, squatter, had matted hair under her Welsh bonnet and wore a miserable plaid shawl around her shoulders. She was called Myfanwy. I felt sorry for her, she seemed like a cuckoo in the nest and, being half Welsh myself, I thought it was quite unfair.

We saw a sign for Grand St Bernard. It makes me think about the St Bernard dog, native of Switzerland. From memory I think they traditionally have a small barrel of brandy hanging from their collar (for medicinal purposes of course) for when they help rescue stranded travellers from an avalanche. That, Diary, is straight off the top of my head, don't quote me on that! Not sure if I like Bernard as a name – apologies to any Bernards out there – I wouldn't call my son Bernard, although names are difficult things to settle on, so many to choose from these days!

We arrive in France, no fanfare or 'Bienvenue' signs, just one announcing we are in Alsace. Our destination is Colmar, a town just a few miles over the border. I decided we should find a supermarket first and get in some essentials – beer and wine mostly, as we are running a bit dry. I asked Sally to take us to a supermarket.

Knowing as I do, that the supermarkets are normally out of town, I was a bit unnerved when Sally took us into the centre of Colmar, down the cobbled streets and through the market. John was surprisingly calm about it; I abandoned Sally and turned her off. It was clear that we couldn't access the supermarket that she had selected for us. By good luck rather than good management, I spotted a sign for LeClerc, my all-time favourite

French supermarket – did I ever tell you, Diary, how much I love a supermarket? I repeat myself sometimes!

The supermarket was only 700 metres from our campsite, so how annoying wasting all that time! That's a black mark for Sally today! My mum used to keep a chart for me and my brother when we were kids, and we were awarded gold stars for good behaviour or black marks for bad – I had mostly stars on my chart and my brother had mostly black marks! In the supermarket, I had a good old browse and managed,

and that some things work out and some things don't, and that I should share all those things with you, Diary.

The swim was very good. Completely different to Italy. A few serious swimmers, all going up and down getting in their lengths. Mind you, the pool is only small, so they were thrashing around and looked very intense. I dipped in and out wearing my bright orange costume. It is rather revealing around the bustline, so I had to take some care, not wishing to reveal my attributes to all and sundry!

at last, to find a swimming costume. It was reduced to seven euros. Granted it was a bit bling, but that tends to be my style anyway. I snapped it up, we paid and off we went to check in at the campsite.

It was very hot by now; I was into my new costume in no time, as I wanted to have my daily swim. On that subject, I have still a 100 percent record, as I have been in water every day that there has been some available to me. My eldest daughter, Kit, called me up at that point, and I told her I had a new costume on. She was saying how proud she was of me making this journey and keeping my diary up to date and doing the swimming. She spurred me on, and I have renewed enthusiasm. She reminds me everything is a learning curve,

Back to the motorhome. John snoozed outside while I prepared our meal. Tonight's dinner involved leftovers. Using cooked potatoes from last night's raclette and the remaining hot dog sausages, I cobbled together a bit of a nod to a choucroute. The storm clouds were gathering once again, rumbling from the heavens. We just managed to eat our dinner outside before those heavens opened and the rain came, and we hastily packed the table and chairs away and settled down indoors.

Another good day. We are thinking of hiring electric bikes tomorrow, weather permitting, which will be a great thing to do – it's years since I have been on a saddle!

Bon nuit!

— *Day 23 Recipe* —
HOT-DOG CHOUCROUTE HASH

Smoked sausages are extremely popular in this area, and I make this camping-friendly dish with a strong nod to Strasbourg and Alsace. Any sausage will work, but I just used a jar of hot-dog ones for ease. I included some cabbage and some mustard, together with honey and white-wine vinegar to get that choucroute feel.

Ingredients (serves 2)

- 2 tablespoons oil
- 1 onion, finely chopped
- Cooked and cooled sliced potatoes *(the size of two large baking potatoes or 10 new potatoes, unpeeled)*
- 3 garlic cloves, crushed
- 500g hot-dog sausages, sliced into chunks
- 2 handfuls savoy style cabbage, sliced
- 1 teaspoon caraway/fennel seeds *(optional)*
- 2 tablespoons cider or white-wine vinegar
- 1 tablespoon honey
- 1 tablespoon wholegrain mustard
- Salt and pepper
- Drizzle of American yellow mustard
- Drizzle of ketchup
- Fresh dill/chives to garnish

Method

In a large frying pan, heat the oil and cook the onions for a few minutes until soft. Add the cooked potatoes and sauté until starting to crisp.

Add the garlic, sausages, and cabbage and sauté for a few minutes. Stir in the herbs.

Mix the honey, wholegrain mustard and vinegar in a bowl and then add to the pan. Stir through and season with salt and pepper.

Drizzle over a little ketchup and yellow mustard. Scatter over the green herbs and serve.

Some people wanted champagne and caviar when they should have had beer and hot dogs.

Dwight D. Eisenhower

– *Day* 24 –

COLMAR,
HAUT-RHIN

Today was all about bikes, Diary. We bit the bullet and splashed the cash to hire two electric bikes from the reception here at the campsite in Colmar. We have seen that there are cycle paths around here, so we decided it should be safe enough to navigate and get to see a bit further afield. The first thing I'll say about it is that, in principle, investing in a couple of e-bikes to take on a tour would be a good idea. However, I would buy a different style of handlebars. These French bikes I found very difficult to steer and stay in control of. It felt very high up, and I can imagine it was a similar

but could we find the path? Fed up and narky, we decided to abandon that mission and head to Colmar.

Once in the centre of Colmar, we locked up the bikes and strolled around the streets. It is a beautiful town, with old buildings that are mostly half-timbered. It reminded me of the Pied Piper story – I know he was in Hamelin, and I have never been there, but if I was location scouting, Colmar would do for the Pied Piper blockbuster! We found a tourist office and asked about the canal path. 'Oh, yes,' said the assistant,

feeling riding a penny farthing. I had a good few wobbles and near misses. However, they were great to get from A to B without exerting too much effort.

We had a little map from the campsite showing us potential routes. We decided to try the route along the canal. It said it was about 10 kilometres of path, and we would see vineyards and nature at its best. We strapped our helmets on and off we went. Around and around we went, trying to find the path that ran down the canal bank. We could see the canal,

'here it is' and started to draw the route with a highlighter pen. We studied the route; it was exactly where we were in the morning! We decided to go back and try again.

Back at the canal. This time we dismount our trusty steeds and inspect the area more closely. There is a path, which has a dead-end sign, but we cycled down it. It was not 10 kilometres, nor did we see any vineyards, but we did see a bit of life and nature. We saw a few houseboats and a barge, we saw two fishermen, a jogger, and I saw a large bird flying towards us (I thought perhaps an owl, but it was midday, not midnight, so probably not) and we then came to the dead-end. We returned along a different path, one that ran adjacent to the motorway, but high up, so we were looking down on the traffic – well, we couldn't help but look down being sat on those bikes, honestly, talk about on top of the world!

from the pool as it could be (maybe half a mile), so it was great to zoom along on the bike. The swim was a bit annoying today, as there were lots of pre-pubescent girls squealing and splashing around. I waited until they had wandered off, before having a dip. I got chatting to a couple from Sheffield. We identified as being from the same tribe very quickly, funny

We called at my favourite supermarket again and I went looking for another bargain-basement swimming costume. The cheapest ones were not in my size, so I bought a slightly more expensive and more modest style of costume than yesterday's all-revealing one, and we cycled back to the campsite.

We were both exhausted. You do need to pedal e-bikes, they are not like my mum's mobility scooter that glides along without any effort. We had a nap. Remember, John and I are always up at cock-crow, so by lunchtime we have put a shift in already! When I awoke, I decided to go and swim in my new costume. I cycled off up to the pool, as our pitch is as far away

how that happens – I knew immediately that they were not Dutch, nor French, nor German, but they were Yorkshire. They were great and very chilled out, even though their motorhome had conked out in the middle of a French hamlet yesterday. They had knocked on a door for help and a lady in her 80s answered. With the help of Google translate they got the van fixed. It cost them 1,000 euros. I winced at that, but they said: 'It could have been worse!' John joined me and went into the pool too, a rare occurrence.

Now on the way back, Diary, I put my shorts and towel in my backpack and I cycled in only my costume. I feel this was a pivotal moment in the trip, perhaps in my life. I know what you must be thinking, how can cycling half a mile in a swimsuit be significant? During many periods of my life, I have been ashamed of my body, and always hid behind towels or sarongs on the beach, or at the pool. Even on this holiday I have done it. Out of nowhere, perhaps just 'the wind beneath

reminds me of Vanessa, my youngest daughter. Born a second child, when the first was eight years old, she was always around older people, like her big sister and her pals and our friends in France when we had the house there. She was always able to converse with adults as a child and, certainly by the time she was a teenager, Vanessa was completely

my wings' feeling, speeding along on the bike in the late afternoon sunshine emboldened me. I asked John to take a photo, full body and looking straight into the lens. There, I feel it, I will not body-shame myself again, we have one life!

I prepared supper, just something light tonight. It was garlic mushrooms on toast, truly scrumptious and hit the spot. Quick too, as it only takes 10 minutes to prepare and cook. Once we had eaten, I sat for a while with a glass of chilled wine. I watched a group opposite – clearly a few couples have met up for the weekend. They are cooking at a BBQ and I spot a teenage girl with them who is laying the table. She

comfortable sitting and chatting with anyone, just like the girl I was watching tonight. My dad always said: 'She is no shop egg that one' (an unusual turn of phrase!), referring to Vanessa. I wish all her grandparents had lived to see her achievements: Dr Vanessa Wright PhD, MSt, MA, BA Hons, they would have been proud. At least my mum is still around.

It's been a good day, Diary, we are on a roll. Tomorrow, we move again, but not very far this time, up towards Strasbourg. In another week we shall be home. It's going too fast, so I'm trying to make all the memories I can.

– *Day 24 Recipe* –
CHAMPIGNONS DU PARIS ON TOAST

Champignons du Paris are large button mushrooms, named after Paris, as so many were discovered growing when the metro was being constructed. Now these fungi are mostly grown in the Loire valley. This recipe is so quick, but totally lush – you could easily serve this as a starter or a light lunch.

Ingredients (serves 2)

- Knob of butter and splash of olive oil
- 12 mushrooms, thickly sliced
- 4 garlic cloves, crushed
- Salt and pepper
- 1 teaspoon wholegrain mustard
- 50ml white wine
- 100ml double cream
- 2 tablespoons cheese (*I used parmesan, but cheddar is good*)
- Squeeze of lemon juice
- Thick slices of baguette griddled and drizzled with olive oil, or a toasted crumpet!
- Fresh parsley to garnish

Method

Melt the butter and oil in a frying pan and add the mushrooms. Cook for a few minutes until they start to soften, shrink, give off their juices and take on a little colour.

Add the garlic, mustard, salt and pepper and continue to cook over a moderate heat for a few minutes.

Pour in the wine and cook until most of the liquid has gone. Add the cream and the cheese, and stir through.

Serve on top of the toast and garnish with parsley.

Why did the mushroom go to the party? Because he's a fungi!

Louis Tomlinson

It was a day of two halves today, Diary. We moved sites again from Colmar up to Saverne, which is in the countryside but not a million miles from Strasbourg. It was a journey of just over an hour, so we were not in a mad rush to leave. I made a very scrumptious and interesting sandwich for breakfast; I know sandwiches can be a bit boring, but this one has a back-story. My daughter Vanessa's partner Charles once had a sandwich when he was on a work trip to Freiburg im Breisgau, in Germany. He likes to

describe it as the best sandwich he ever had – a pretzel-shaped individual bread, filled with smoked ham, cheese, slices of tomato and mustard. The combination of the fillings with the salt-encrusted bread dough apparently cannot be matched. I wanted to recreate the Charles Whalley sandwich. I did, and it was sublime!

It was a fabulous drive to the next site. I was unfamiliar with this side of France, and it is magnificent in quite an understated way – is that a contradiction? The landscape today included mountains, low and green, with the Vosges in the far distance. Closer, there were cornfields, almost ready to harvest, golden in the sunshine, their ears wafting in the gentle breeze. Next to them were green fields of maize, not yet as high as an elephant's eye (do you remember that song from *Oklahoma*?). These were planted in such a way that it formed a chequerboard effect that was very pleasing to the eye. The

The place names are very Germanic. This makes me think of the war again, as this part of France must have been occupied early on. It also makes me think of my friend, Karen. Karen's dad was called Rudi Richter – what a terrific name! He was German and was taken as a prisoner of war.

He saw his war out in East Yorkshire in a camp that is now the Eden Camp museum. He never went back to Germany,

villages were still half-timbered, and there were countless small castles on top of hills, looking down and protecting the terrain.

I saw two herons that appeared to be soaring on the thermals. I thought back three weeks to our stay in Burgundy, and that heron stalking its prey. I suppose they are territorial, and fish in the same places all their lives. We saw vines everywhere and sunflowers, their droopy, heavy heads bobbing around in the breeze.

and after he was released, he met Karen's mum and settled in Yorkshire. I was a bit terrified of him when I was a child, because his English was very heavily accented, and for years when we knocked on their back door, he would often shout something so guttural that we couldn't make it out. 'Shut the bloody vindoff' is the phrase I remember most; I think it meant shut the window! As an adult, I really hit it off with Rudi, and he was sorely missed in the community when he died.

As we turned onto the small roads leading to our campsite, we saw young girls with a trestle table selling cherries. Then we saw a man doing the same. Cherries must be local here; I wonder if they make regional specialities with them?

not totally happy with the pitch to reception, but we decided to take it. I had a fabulous swim in the covered pool, just perfect really. I went back to the van to encourage John to come out and play.

When we arrived at the campsite, we got a great first impression. Well kept, peaceful, with a small pool and a snack bar. We had been allocated an emplacement (pitch), which is often the case. Unfortunately, it was not a good one – not a blade of grass, but rather rough shingle full of weeds and cigarette ends. It backs on to the snack bar. It does have a view, so long as nobody else takes the pitch next to us. I mention that we're

He did come and have a swim, and he was very enamored with the pretty blue dragonfly that kept perching on his big toe as he dried off on a deckchair.

After the swim, the afternoon stretched out in front of us. I walked around the site and saw umpteen beautifully located empty pitches. I was puzzled… Why did we have this dodgy pitch? I was a wee bit rattled. Anyway, I still had a nice view from ours. I set up my cooking station to make recipe number 25 and had just taken my first photograph when a big motorhome drove straight on to the pitch next door, blocking the whole view and all the sunshine. A German family, staying for just the night. Diary, I thought: 'That's it, I must do something!' Still wearing my apron, I went back to reception. I explained my predicament, and that I needed a better pitch – one where

THE 'CHARLES WHALLEY' SANDWICH

I could work and take photographs. I told them about the book I am writing. I ask if we can move tomorrow to the pitch where the German family are, as that way I can ensure I keep a view. The receptionist agrees, but with a bit of an attitude.

Dinner was tasty, but it felt a bit of a dud due to the location. The high point for John was that he bought some fries from the snack bar that we share our pitch with, to eat alongside the Coq au Riesling. I must admit, they were good fries, red hot and salty. Take the pleasures where you can!

Also, Diary, and this is between you and I, I hadn't been feeling too well the last couple of hours today – just one of those things. I don't have antibiotics or any medication, so I just drank glass upon glass of water to help fix the problem. It did eventually work, but it was gone midnight when I felt able to write to you and share my woes. I feel OK now though, so I need to catch some sleep. Tomorrow is another day!

– Day 25 Recipe –
COQ AU RIESLING

This is the Alsace version of chicken chasseur. Made with Riesling white wine, mushrooms and cream. Generally, the chicken is cooked with skin and on the bone, but to make it more campsite-friendly here, I used boneless and skinless chicken thighs. If you can't find those in the supermarkets, you can use chicken breast, or use thighs with skin and on the bone. You must allow a longer cooking time if it's on the bone, and simmer for a good hour. For browning the chicken, you can give it a quick burst on the gas BBQ if you have one, otherwise just do it in the pan, as it says below. If you can't get Riesling, any dry white wine will do fine.

Ingredients (serves 2)

- Tablespoon of oil or butter
- Four skinless and boneless chicken thighs
- 1 onion, finely sliced
- 6 large mushrooms, thickly sliced
- 4 cloves of garlic, crushed
- 1 tablespoon dried thyme
- 1 tablespoon Dijon mustard
- 1 tablespoon plain flour
- 250ml chicken stock
- 250ml Riesling wine
- 100ml double cream
- Salt and pepper
- Chopped parsley to garnish

Method

Heat the butter or oil in a large frying pan. Brown the chicken on both sides, for about five minutes in total.

Add the onion and mushrooms and cook until soft, then add the garlic, thyme, mustard, and flour. Give it a good mix and then add the stock.

On quite a high heat, bring the mixture to a boil and then reduce to a soft, rolling boil*, and cook until the stock has reduced a little, and the sauce has thickened. This will take about five minutes.

Add the wine, bring to a boil again and then reduce to a rolling boil* to thicken the sauce once more. It will likely take about 10 to 15 minutes. The sauce should be thick.

Stir through the cream, and season with salt and pepper to taste. Garnish with parsley.

It is excellent served with pasta, rice or mashed potatoes.

A rolling boil is more than a simmer, but less than a full boil. This is to get the dish cooked in 30 minutes. If you are not in a rush, just simmer it and chill out!

Wine...
the intellectual
part of the meal.
Alexandre Dumas

– Day 26 –
SAVERNE,
BAS-RHIN

What a difference a day makes, 24 little hours – do you know that song, Diary? I have been singing it and changing the words to 'what a difference a pitch makes'. As soon as the German family departed this morning (and they were off good and early) we moved on to that pitch. It has made a massive difference to me – it has a good outlook and is nice and level. I can't explain it properly, but it has lifted my spirits.

This done, and all reset on the new pitch, we went up to reception to collect our pre-ordered baguette and pay for some hired bikes. We decided that electric bikes would enable

us to get down into the town and look around, and possibly ride along another canal, hopefully for a bit further than we did at Colmar.

I set off full of confidence. I was riding downhill on what I thought was a cycle path, when I very nearly collided with a car that was turning left into my path. I mean, I had about a metre's notice to brake and avoid a nasty accident. Rattled, I carried on, and down and down we went to the bottom of the hill. I clocked that it was not a lazy Sunday morning in Saverne – there was a Brocante taking place down by the canal. A Brocante is a flea market/antique market, call it what you will, it is often a mixture of good old stuff and junk. Anyway, we decided to head for it, and as I was making a slight turn to mount a tiny kerb (only two inches), I lost my balance and crashed to the floor, the bike straddled across me. They are heavy things due to them being motorised. Fortunately, and count your blessings where you can, I was on the pavement and not on the road, but I was upset and cried a bit.

up on their own doorstep, and it's a great social thing, all the neighbours passing by for a chat and a poke through the stuff. When we had our place in Parsac, and we owned it nigh on 20 years, our fête patronale was the last weekend in August. A few days before the weekend started, the bunting would go up and small fairground rides, rifle ranges and hook-a-ducks were set up by the primary school. A beer tent and a small

It's always important to keep safe wherever you are, but a concern of mine has been that if anything happened to me on this trip, John and I might find it difficult to manage the situation. I don't want to over-egg it, but it is always a worry. Anyway, onwards to the Brocante.

Most French towns and villages have an annual fête, which usually includes a Brocante, where the streets are lined with people trying to sell items (mostly junk) on a trestle table: old toys, books, records, calendars from 1972, horrible stuffed weasels, nuts and bolts and screwdrivers, farm machinery, old clothes, furniture. Quite often, if it is in a village, the folk set

stage were erected. On the Sunday we had the Brocante, and at some point during the afternoon the local brass band, led by our postman playing his saxophone, would march through the street (not streets, as there was only the one!). A troupe of folk dancers wearing clogs would stomp around on the stage, and the local bar and the beer tent would be packed out – quite a spectacle, as the rest of the year the place was as dead as a nit.

Traditions and stories are built up over time, and we had our own fun on the fête weekend. John and I would invite family and friends to join us for the week, as we could easily accommodate 13 guests, more if we made up beds on the floor.

Anyway, one of the things we did was to set a challenge for the group. Everyone got five euros to spend at the Brocante, and had to buy something that would hopefully win the competition for the most tasteless object. We all set off to scout around the stalls. Some made their purchase very

After a cursory look around, as I was still feeling shocked from my fall, we rode back to the site. The most interesting thing at the fête was the carousel from 1900. I love those, and have memories of both my girls riding them. The canal was interesting, as we watched two small cruising boats negotiate the locks.

quickly; others went back throughout the day looking for that special something. The idea was you brought your item back and secretly placed it on a viewing table. After dinner, all the items would be judged by poll, and the winner would be selected. From memory, the most hideous thing that won one year was a cow's hoof that had been lined with faux fur and was re-purposed as a nibbles dish – peanut, anyone?

Back at the motorhome I had a 'Zoom' date. Every few weeks I am a guest on BBC Radio Leeds, and today was the day. They are interested in our story, Diary, and it's really lovely to be invited on. Zoom works well, and I did my 10 minutes of chatter about the trip, my book and food. That done, I made lunch. Today's recipe is tarte flambée – a bit like a pizza, but made with only crème fraiche, cheese and lardons. It is a regional speciality, but you can find them in the chiller cabinets all over France. For ease, I used a wrap as my base. It was dead easy and very moreish.

John had a tinker with his bike. He just couldn't resist: have bike, will tinker! I think he just adjusted the saddle and then he rode off into the afternoon sun! After my lunch settled, I went off to the pool again. There are quite a few Brits on this site, like us, booked via the Caravan and Motorhome Club. I had a smashing chat by the pool with a couple from Wigan,

lady set up a portable kitchen in the snack-bar area and her blackboard offered paella, fries, drinks and cake. Next, a food van arrived selling crêpes. For a quiet site, it was quite busy and interesting to watch everything, especially the cheese man interacting with his customers and selling his wares. I was out of cash, otherwise I would have made a purchase.

As the trip is drawing close to the end, I wanted to use up some coq au vin from the recipe I made on day 3, from

Colin and Sue – they told me their story and I really enjoyed chatting, which is part of this type of holiday, the bonding with others over shared interests.

Once back outside the van, as the weather was so splendid, I just sat, drink in hand. Interesting things occurred; a local cheesemonger set up his stall opposite us – only in France would you get a pop-up cheese stall on a campsite! Then a

way back in Burgundy. I had frozen a couple of portions. John went to buy some more fries from the lady with the blackboard. Twice in two days we had chips – bloody lovely they were too, Diary, malt vinegar and salt, perfect!

I think today has been close to perfection. I don't ask much, just warm sun, a good pitch, good company and good health. Going to bed now, feeling good!

– Day 26 Recipe –
TARTE FLAMBÉE

This is kind of the French version of pizza. Tarte flambée is very popular in the Alsace region, but you can buy it in shops all over the country. Normally, it is an unleavened bread base, topped with Emmental cheese, lardons and crème fraiche, and it is oven-baked. For my cheat version I used a tortilla wrap, which is toasted gently in a frying pan. So crisp and scrumptious!

Ingredients (serves 1)

- A little oil
- Tortilla wrap
- Handful smoked lardons or chopped bacon
- Grated or finely sliced Emmental cheese *(a piece about the size of a pack of cards)*
- 2 tablespoons full fat crème fraîche

Method

Cook the lardons in the oil until brown and crispy, then remove to a plate and set aside. Gently warm the tortilla on both sides in the pan.

Spread a tablespoon of crème fraîche on the wrap, then add cheese, a little more creme fraiche and a bit more cheese. Scatter the lardons on top.

Gently cook until the cheese has melted, taking care not to burn the bottom of the wrap (use a low heat).

Le bonheurre est dans la cuisine happiness is in the kitchen.

Paul Bocuse

VILLENEUVE-SUR-AISNE,
AISNE

Another travel day today, Diary. Moving north, heading closer and closer to home. We are leaving this very lovely site in Alsace to go to another, a good three-hour drive from where we are now. This area of France is a bit of a mystery to me, as I have not travelled here very much, if at all. I know from history lessons that there has always been a lot of shifting of borders in this region: sometimes it

Anyway, Diary, more of that later. We hit the road, and once more saw rapid changes in the landscape. We started with dense forests of fir trees, very dark green. It was quite windy, but those strong, old firs never shifted at all, unlike us, as we were buffeted around for the first time on this trip. The thick forest soon gave way to more of a rolling landscape, with those pretty church spires that remind me so much of Christmas

has been French, sometimes German, but it is French now. When I hear the word Alsace, I think of Alsatian dogs – I had a framed picture of one on my bedroom wall when I was a kid. I remember even then not knowing why it was on my wall, because as far as I know we didn't have any connection with Alsatians! When I think of this part of the world, I'm also reminded of quiche Lorraine, one of my favourites – who doesn't love a quiche? Even John will have a slice at a push. So that's what I decided to make for today's recipe: my nod to a quiche Lorraine. I have not used the motorhome oven on this trip, not even once – it's still gleaming new. Instead, I made my 'quiche' in a frying pan. In reality, it's closer to a frittata, and it was great to use up bits and pieces in the fridge before we get to the real tail end of the trip.

cards – no snow in evidence of course, but I think how pretty this would be in winter. We had the cornfields again, this time in the process of being harvested, then we were in the rural, fertile flatlands and I noticed crops of potatoes that signalled to me we were getting to the north.

I saw the road signs telling me we were in Lorraine, then back in Alsace. We saw signs for Metz and Nancy, both places that remind me of people. I have never been to Metz, but my oldest friend, Caroline, was placed there for half of her year abroad when she was studying modern languages at university (she went to Bremen for the other half). I remember being excited to get her letters, as we corresponded all the time she was away, and I was very proud of her. She went to university, I got married and got a job in a bank. I remember being captivated by her lifestyle living in Metz.

Nancy, now then. A girl's name as old as the Bible, plus it is that big city in northern France. I have known two Nancys in my life and both were formidable women. The first was

my neighbour, who, along with her husband, Eddie, looked after little Katharine when she was a baby – they were in their late sixties even then. They, along with my Auntie Anne, shared the childcare so I could go out to work. I will always be indebted to them, but they have all passed away now of course. Nancy was quite scary, but would do anything for me. She had been a dinner lady at the local school, and I think she terrified the kids. My cousin Janet, who went to that school, confirms this to be the case! It seems like that was part of the job description of being a good dinner lady in the 1960s: 'Clear your plate or no pudding!'

The other Nancy was my mother in-law. Again, not a woman to take any prisoners, and you had to know her to love her. I

came to love her despite her rather hearty vocabulary – she could swear like a trooper! She was so kind underneath, with a heart of gold. She welcomed Katharine to her bosom, and when Vanessa was born, well, she was made up with an unexpected addition to the family. Nancy had the most amazing eyes; steely blue and they could flash like darts. John inherited a green version of those eyes. At her funeral we had the Frank Sinatra song 'Nancy with the Flashing Eyes' played as we left the crematorium. It seemed to fit the occasion.

Anyway, Diary, back to today's journey. I saw the river Moselle, as well as signs for Moselle wine, although I didn't see any vineyards. We went past part of the Maginot line, which I know was a very long fortification built in the 1930s on the French border with Belgium, Luxembourg, Germany, Switzerland and Italy in an attempt to keep France safe from invasion in the future. I think that is the case, but once again my knowledge is a bit sketchy – I have got lots to read up on whilst I'm here. I then saw a sign for the river Meuse. Again I have a little story for you, Diary: when I was about 19, my mum bought me one of those painted mirrors, like you often see in pubs. Mine had an art nouveau painting on it, of a woman with flowers in her hair, and the writing said 'Bières de la Meuse'. I love that mirror, and when my daughter Katharine was small, she thought the lady depicted was me!

A few years ago, the string it was hanging on snapped, and the mirror crashed down and broke into smithereens. I cried for days! I was so sad about the loss of that mirror. However, that Christmas my family presented me with a new one. They had searched eBay for months and finally found one. It hangs pride of place in my lounge now (with a much more secure fastening!). Maybe we should have stopped somewhere in Meuse for a beer to recreate the picture on the mirror – next time!

Eventually we arrived at Villeneuve-sur-Aisne, a small village yet to be investigated by me. That is planned for tomorrow. However, I called the chemist to buy something to help with my ailment. I winced at the price, just short of 13 euros, and I can see from the ingredients it's just herbal stuff, not an

antibiotic or anything powerful to zap the bug! I bought some cranberry juice to wash the tablets down. Fingers crossed! This is another good campsite. The pitches are huge, really massive, with enough space that we can have a game of boules on our pitch tomorrow. I enjoyed my daily swim – it was quiet at the pool, with just me and another lady floating about. The water was beautiful, just the perfect temperature.

I was very tired tonight, so I was thankful that the recipe for dinner was a quick one. All my recipes are on the speedy side, but this one could almost cook itself. I made the quiche Lorraine frittata, and I added some potatoes (hurrah from John) and tomatoes, so it is not totally authentic (as the quiche has just bacon, eggs, cream and cheese), but what the heck. We enjoyed it with a crusty loaf.

It is time for bed now. I'm looking forward to a steady day of resting and pottering about tomorrow. I wish you goodnight, Diary!

– Day 27 Recipe –
'NOD' TO QUICHE LORRAINE

I think if you surveyed 100 people and asked them to name a quiche, it would likely be a unanimous answer, quiche Lorraine. I felt that I couldn't spend time in this area and not cook something Lorraine-related.

I have taken the basic filling of bacon, eggs and cream and made a stove-top version. I added other things that I had handy; it is a good one for using up things as you head home from your trip. A cross between a crustless quiche, an omelette and a frittata.

Ingredients (serves 1)

- 2 tablespoons oil
- 10 salad potatoes, cooked, cooled and thickly sliced
- 4 thick rashers of bacon (or pack of lardons), chopped
- 1 red onion, sliced into rings
- 3 eggs
- 100ml cream
- Handful cherry tomatoes, halved
- Handful grated cheese
- Salt and pepper

Method

Heat the oil in a frying pan and then sauté the potatoes until golden.

Add the chopped-up bacon/lardons and the onion and cook for a couple of minutes. Season with salt and pepper.

Make a couple of wells in the mixture and carefully crack two of the eggs into the wells. Keep cooking on a moderate heat. When the eggs have started to cook and the egg white has started to set, add the tomatoes to the mixture.

Beat the third egg with the cream, and pour over the mixture in the pan (it will not completely cover the mixture). Reduce the heat to prevent the egg and cream mixture from burning.

Scatter over the cheese and adjust the seasoning if required. Placing a lid on the pan will help cook the eggs.

Serve once the eggs are set.

The romance alas waned and withered, but the quiche lived on!

Roald Dahl

— Day 28 —

VILLENEUVE-SUR-AISNE,
AISNE

I felt tons better this morning, refreshed and looking forward to the day. We didn't have much planned, and it is such a small place we just went for a wander up to the small town, along the river and back to the campsite. The village used to be called Guignicourt, but a few years ago they changed the name to Villeneuve-sur-Aisne. That confused

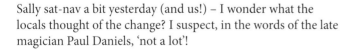

Sally sat-nav a bit yesterday (and us!) – I wonder what the locals thought of the change? I suspect, in the words of the late magician Paul Daniels, 'not a lot'!

Anyway, it was very pleasant indeed. The usual clutch of amenities, a small but perfectly formed supermarket (except they didn't sell Bratwurst, which I needed for tonight), and a beautiful church that was huge for a town so small, with turrets that made it look part fairytale castle. There was a war

memorial, a tabac, selling cigarettes, newspapers and stuff like that, a bar with a plat du jour menu outside, and a gorgeous boulangerie that I had spotted when we drove by yesterday, but unfortunately it was closed today. Finally, we walked past the Mairie (the town hall) and not forgetting the Salle de Fêtes which is a bit like a community centre. I noticed a poster

saying there had been a pétanque match a few days ago, so all in all a thriving little town.

I took quite a lot of photographs; it is amazing what you can find when you snap, when you turn your eyes into a camera lens and see things through the eyes of any potential readers of my book. On the return to the campsite, we walked along the riverbank. The river Aisne was very still, and the water was green, though not an unpleasant shade. Massive trees with heavy branches overhung the river, making it quite hard to see very much in places. We found a couple of places though, where there were some very old wooden rowing boats – wide with flat bottoms – with old steps leading down to them from the riverbank. The boats were chained to tree trunks, and great lily pads were floating all around the boats. We walked

on and came across an elderly French couple. The chap was wet right up to his armpits and his backside was covered in filthy slime –well not his bare backside, he was wearing trousers! His wife spoke to me in rapid French. I figured out he had been going to fish, but had slipped into the river. He was unhurt and fine, but quite indignant – they were packing up his fishing tackle and calling it quits, I think.

Once back at the motorhome, I made us a bite of lunch. Sometimes, Diary, the simplest of things are the best. I sliced up a tomato and sprinkled it with salt, leaving it to warm up in the sunshine and release some of its juices. A slice of baguette, spread with a little mayo and topped with the tomatoes – so tasty and fresh and I really enjoyed it.

We did have a game of boules on our extra-large pitch. I am not that fond of the game, most likely because I am rubbish at it! Anyway, John enjoyed it, winning every round. We packed the boules away for another day and then it was time for my swim. This time I was delighted that John decided to join me – it is quite remarkable how many times he has been in the pool

this trip. We had our house in France for 20 years and he only went in the pool once or twice! Funny though, how today he asked if he had another pair of trunks somewhere (which he hasn't), as apparently he hates the ones he has been wearing all the holiday!

When we got back to the pitch and were sitting in the sunshine to dry off properly, loads of UK-plate motorhomes and caravans turned up in convoy. I got the impression they were all together, perhaps in some sort of rally. The site seemed quite full to me, but still it was very quiet and chilled out. The evening approached at speed – where the day went today, Diary, I just don't know. I was thinking that I haven't missed the television at all, I had not even thought about it.

All part of the package of being away from home for me, I know some folks bring a portable, but I can't be bothered with it.

Dinner tonight is supposed to be bratwurst sausages cooked in wheat beer and onions, and served with stoemp. Stoemp is a type of mashed potato, a bit like champ or bubble and squeak, in that it has other vegetables mixed through it – in this case some carrot and leek. As I said, the supermarket didn't have bratwurst (I should have tried a Lidl somewhere, as for sure they always sell them), but anyway, it doesn't really matter what sausages are used, it is more about the beer and onion gravy. I bought some Toulouse sausages, totally the wrong end of the country, as Toulouse is in the south-west, but what the heck, they caught my eye and were fat and porky.

I cooked the whole lot outside, which was great. Sometimes it has been too scorchio to do that, but it's far cooler here in the north, and cooking en plein air feels fabulous. I have practised all my recipes at home many

times and had other people try them out to make sure they work. This is one of my favourites, as it's real comfort food. It goes without saying that this dish met with John's full approval, and he got what was left in the bottle of beer to drink – it was over 7 per cent proof so he should get some good sleep tonight!

Speaking of sleep, I am so tired again. This trip has been full-on, and perhaps because I know it is nearing the end, I feel a bit floppy. Another early night tonight as we continue our journey, the last leg of travel tomorrow, right across the top slice of France, heading towards the ferry port. A good day though, now one of so many. I bid you goodnight, see you in the morning!

BRATWURST IN BEER WITH STOEMP

Let's start by saying that you don't need bratwurst specifically for this recipe. Any sausages will work, but ideally fat, porky and herby! I tried it with vegetarian sausages too and it came out great.

This is a French/Belgian/German fusion dish. In northern France, close to the Belgian and German borders, stoemp is a very common dish. Root vegetables, leeks, onions, all cooked, mashed and then fried to crisp up a little bit. You can use leftover cooked veg, as with bubble and squeak.

Ingredients (serves 2)

Stoemp
- 1 tablespoon oil
- 1 leek, finely sliced
- 2 big potatoes, unpeeled but finely diced
- 2 carrots, unpeeled but finely diced
- Salt and pepper
- 1 teaspoon nutmeg *(optional)*
- Large knob of butter

Sausages
- 1 tablespoon oil
- 4 fat bratwurst/pork/vegetarian sausages
- 2 onions, finely sliced into rings
- 1 teaspoon wholegrain mustard
- 1 teaspoon smoked paprika
- 1 stock cube *(beef or vegetable)*
- 1 tablespoon plain flour
- 500ml wheat beer
- Salt and pepper

Method

Stoemp

Cook the leek in oil for a few minutes until it is tender, and then remove to a plate.

Fill a large pan with boiling water and add a teaspoon of salt. Place the diced potatoes and carrot into the pan and bring to a rolling boil*. Place a lid on the pan and cook for about 20 minutes until tender.

Drain, and crush roughly with a fork or spoon (we are not looking for a smooth mash), return to the pan and stir through the cooked leeks. Add the knob of butter and the nutmeg, and season well with salt and pepper.

Sausages

Heat the oil in a frying pan and brown the sausages, then remove to a plate.

Cook the sliced onions in the pan on a gentle heat until they are soft and translucent. Add the mustard, stock cube and the smoked paprika and stir in.

Sprinkle over the flour and mix well. Pour in the beer and bring to a boil.

Return the sausages to the pan and reduce the heat to a rolling boil*. Cook until the beer has reduced by about half. Season to taste with salt and pepper.

* A rolling boil is more than a simmer, but less than a full boil. This is to get the dish cooked in 30 minutes. If you are not in a rush, just simmer it and chill out!

If I have any vice it is eating. If I was told I could only have one food for the rest of my life, I could put up with sausage and mash forever.

Tom Baker

– Day 29 –
GUÎNES,
PAS-DE-CALAIS

Today we were up and away in good time. We waved goodbye to this very pretty area and an especially lovely campsite on the Aisne, and began making our final journey on the homeward leg of our trip. The sun was playing out – we have been very fortunate with the weather Diary, don't you think?

We hit the autoroute, and Sally was telling us that this road would take us within 20km of our final site. I set up some more tunes from Spotify, as it was a straightforward drive, so we could relax and maybe sing a little. First up we had a bit of Cat Stevens. I Googled him to see when he changed his name to Yusef, and I discovered how he became spiritual, and

that he is half Greek Cypriot – fancy that. We moved on to Queen, and as we both knew the words, we were singing away like a cat's chorus, 'Scaramouch, Scaramouch, will you do the Fandango' and so on!

The journey to Guînes, which is just a few miles inland from Calais, took about two and a half hours. As I've said already it was a very straightforward drive, and we should have given Sally the day off really. The landscape quickly changed from the gentle prettiness of Lorraine to the rather flat and vacuous area of Hauts-de-France – an area of agriculture, arable I should say, as there was a distinct lack of livestock to be seen. Field upon field of potatoes with their pretty white flowers bobbing around, plus even more fields of corn, wheat, barley and rye. Lots of bread and beer to be made around here I should think.

We travelled along through a blanket of low, grey skies. I saw lots of slag heaps, as there was a big coal-mining industry

old mum, who was about 4ft 6in, with a face like a walnut, and always dressed in black, used to fly out to visit them in rotation, keeping an eye on her far-flung offspring.

We pass fields of electricity-generating turbines; funny how we just accept them now and hardly register their presence. They

around here at one time. This makes me think of the people in my life who have moved from faraway towns, or even countries, to find work in coal mines. Historically, you often had to go where the work was, although I'm sure it is the same for some industries even now. In the 1870s, my paternal grandfather, Josiah, moved from Staffordshire to Yorkshire when he was a teenager with his parents, siblings, aunts, uncles, cousins, grandparents, old Uncle Tom Cobley and all, to settle where the new pits were opened. In my family's case, that was Featherstone, West Yorkshire. Although, slightly closer to where we were passing today though, I think of my old Greek boyfriend, as two of his brothers moved from northern Greece to work in coal mines: one to Germany and one to Belgium. That must have been a culture shock! Their

make me think of my mum. As a very tall-for-her-age girl at 5ft 8¾in (the three-quarters being of ultimate importance), she was given the poem *Behold! a giant am I!* to recite at school – the giant in question being a windmill. She can still recite it to this day, very proudly too!

I saw signs for Cambrai, and I thought it sounded like an interesting place, so I looked it up on my phone as we drove along. Technology is incredible, I think! So much interesting history in the Napoleonic and First World Wars.

Learning about Cambrai and World War I made me think about Josiah again. He was one of the lucky ones, in that he at least came back from that atrocious war in one piece (physically at any rate, who knows what went on upstairs). He was a veteran of the Somme; I think I already mentioned that before. This whole area bears the scars of that hideous war. When we worked for the holiday company, we spent two years based not that far from where we passed through today. John

work from time to time. It is always quite full, with many people on their way to their holidays and returning using it as a stopover site, but it has much to recommend it. Gorgeous, well kept, excellent facilities, things to see locally, and a fine-dining restaurant on the site. Once we got set up, which

and I spent quite a bit of our free time visiting the historical sites and the war-grave cemeteries, and even paid our respects at the Armistice Day parade at Compiègne, where the original Armistice was signed in 1918.

On to cheerier things, Diary. We arrived at our destination with ease. The sun was shining, and the campsite looked amazing. This is another of the old sites where we used to

takes no more than five minutes in a motorhome, we went for a mooch around. It was just as I remembered it, everything was the same.

I set up my table for tonight's meal. It is the first time that this has created any real interest on the trip, but I had lots of people stopping by to comment on how attractive my set-up looked. I tell them all about my book, hopefully generating a bit of interest, which can't hurt! I chat to a couple from Halifax, and once again I identify a member of my own Yorkshire tribe as soon as I hear them speak. They were a lovely couple, Wendy and Kev, and ever so friendly, the type of people you could pal up with.

The meal – pork in creamy sauce with apples and cider – was delicious. I cooked up a few sauté potatoes to go with it. Unfortunately, John and I had a minor falling out just after. John got the monk on (that's a Yorkshire saying for the hump) and we spent an hour or two in a huff. I went to walk around the site, and it was so good to see people enjoying themselves, at the bar, restaurant, ping-pong and crazy golf, but I felt a bit forlorn and tearful. Back at the van we did make friends. I told John it felt like we were two strings on a violin that needed tuning – what could be beautiful music was screeching and awful. How are you at violin tuning, Diary?

A mixed bag then today. Like life, it is not all a bed of roses, but do with it what you can and learn from the mistakes. Tomorrow is another day. It is also the last day of this trip, this wonderful opportunity that I am so fortunate to have been able to take advantage of. I am just going to finish this drink – a Bacardi and coke, my favourite – and then I need to get some beauty sleep.

– *Day 29 Recipe* –

CREAMY PORK AND APPLES IN CIDER

This recipe is one that marries lots of ingredients from all around France! Cider and apple from Normandy; champignons de Paris from, well, Paris; a little Dijon mustard from Burgundy; and the leeks, cream, and pork can be anywhere but in this case they bring a taste of Picardy!

This is a delicious dish and goes well with mashed or sautéed potatoes, rice, or even pasta.

Ingredients (serves 2)

- Knob of butter
- Splash of oil
- 2 thick-cut pork-loin steaks, cut into chunks
- 1 leek, sliced
- 1 punnet of mushrooms (*I used champignons de Paris*), halved
- 1 apple, cored and sliced
- 4 cloves of garlic
- 1 tablespoon dried thyme
- 1 tablespoon Dijon mustard
- 1 tablespoon plain flour
- 200ml dry cider
- Salt and pepper
- 100ml double cream
- Parsley to garnish

Method

Heat the oil and butter in a lidded frying pan, add the pork and cook for a few minutes to brown.

Add the leek and mushrooms and cook for a few minutes, Then add the garlic, apple, thyme and mustard. Continue to cook for five minutes, stirring now and then.

Sprinkle over the flour, and mix well. Add the cider, put the lid on and cook for around 10 minutes. Remove the lid and season to taste. Cook until the liquid has reduced, and it is a sauce-like consistency.

Stir though the cream and heat gently. Sprinkle with parsley and serve.

If you are afraid of butter, use cream!

Julia Child

– *Day 30* –
GUÎNES,
PAS-DE-CALAIS

Diary, what a shock to the system it was to wake up this morning and find the weather had changed overnight from the glorious sunshine that we have enjoyed for the entire 30-day trip (barring a few thunderstorms) to a grey and misty, almost foggy today. On our final day too! I'd had plans to make it a cracker.

Not to let the change in the weather dampen my spirits, I suggested we have a run out somewhere to get a few more photographs for the book. The good thing about a motorhome is, if you do need or want to go somewhere, it only takes a few

foggy that we gave up – we couldn't see far in front of the motorhome, let alone see the white cliffs of Dover. Changing plan, we drove down to Blériot Plage, just outside of Calais. This place is famous for being the location from where the first successful cross-Channel aeroplane flight took off in 1909; the aviator was Louis Blériot and the beach was named after him. It was grey and windswept this morning, but the sand is fine and golden and looks as if it stretches for miles.

We decided to head back to the campsite, and went to buy some duty-free on the way. This done, we arrived back

minutes to get organised. Batten down the hatches, shut the roof vents, unplug the electricity cable and off you go. On this occasion we put our yellow reserved-pitch sign up and coiled the cable around it so nobody would bag our spot!

We drove off to the coast, and I wanted to see either Cap Griz-Nez or Cap Blanc-Nez. Two capes, like rocky outcrops, on the Côte d'Opale, which are the closest points of France to England. As we approached the coast, it was so misty and

at the site and settled down for an afternoon inside the motorhome. I took the opportunity to write up some of my notes, as I like to keep up with things and not get a backlog. It was quite nice to settle down with a cup of tea, some weird French Jaffa-cake-type things, and a family-sized bag of salt-and-vinegar crisps.

What was on my mind though, was my swim and my last supper. I set my intentions right at the beginning to swim every day, to be kinder, and to try to live in the moment. The swimming has gone well, and apart from three days (two in Switzerland, where we didn't have a pool, and one day in Tuscany when, by the time we got back from Florence the pool was closed), I have swum every day. I am not having as much success with the other intentions, but swimming is a thumbs-up. Today though, it was raining, and quite hard. Last night people were walking around in shorts and sundresses, but today, by contrast they were in raincoats, or were

missed, but have been thinking of her. She is 89, although she does remarkably well and is very independent, but I normally see her a few times each week, and since her husband, Bob, died three years ago, she has been without a soulmate.

Anyway, enough of that stuff, the main thing this evening was to get that last recipe cooked. There was not a chance of us eating outside, as that pesky rain was still hard at it. I set up my table indoors and cooked on the stove top. It was a simple

scurrying around under umbrellas. I knew the pool closed at 6.00pm, but I kept putting off going, and I really didn't fancy it at all! At 5.30, I grabbed my stuff and I went to the pool. Diary, I am so pleased with myself that I did that! I didn't give up, I stuck to my intention and felt wonderful for it. That's a good lesson there for me to take forward.

When I got back to the motorhome, I felt a renewed sense of purpose. I wanted this last day to be a good one. In some respects, the poor weather seemed fitting – it was telling me the holiday was over and it was time to return home and put things in order there. I have missed my mum, or not so much

last supper: pancakes filled with lardons, mushrooms, spinach and cheese. Although we are not in Picardy, we are not far away here, so it seemed fitting to call it a Picardy pancake. Catchy, eh?

The hardest part was getting some decent photographs. John was decidedly grumpy about it this evening and I had to really cajole him to cooperate. I know it has been hard every day, spending so much time taking pics of food, but it is paying off and we have some crackers. We ended up with a few good ones. The one I liked most was when I tossed the pancake and it flipped in front of my face, covering my face entirely like a big yellow full moon, which made us both laugh our heads off.

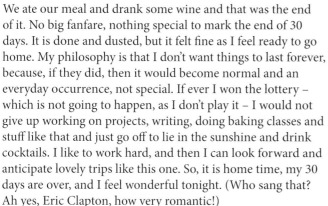

We ate our meal and drank some wine and that was the end of it. No big fanfare, nothing special to mark the end of 30 days. It is done and dusted, but it felt fine as I feel ready to go home. My philosophy is that I don't want things to last forever, because, if they did, then it would become normal and an everyday occurrence, not special. If ever I won the lottery – which is not going to happen, as I don't play it – I would not give up working on projects, writing, doing baking classes and stuff like that and just go off to lie in the sunshine and drink cocktails. I like to work hard, and then I can look forward and anticipate lovely trips like this one. So, it is home time, my 30 days are over, and I feel wonderful tonight. (Who sang that? Ah yes, Eric Clapton, how very romantic!)

I have set my alarm, Diary – don't let me sleep in. We must get up at 6.00am to head off to catch our ferry home. I shall say goodnight now and catch up with you first thing tomorrow!

The next morning...
We did it, up with the larks and off to the ferry. This morning was beautiful, the sunrise was so bright and gorgeous, which

was so very welcome, as it made us feel very cheery as we drove to get the ferry. We checked in with no bother and we headed up to the outside deck to take in the last views of France as we chugged away. I do so love France, and I know it will not be long before we meet again. Oh no, I feel a Vera Lynn song is about to take over my brain and then I'll be singing that all day long: 'We'll meet again, don't know where, don't know when, but I know we'll meet again some sunny day.'

On the boat, we went for the full English again. You know, it wasn't half bad on this return trip. There wasn't much difference, but they served it on better plates this time than they did on the trip out. I find it really makes all the difference how food is served you know, as you eat with your eyes. Anyway, that full English signals that we're heading back to home turf, with just a quick detour to Brighton before we head back north to sunny Yorkshire!

After 30 days of adventures, ups and downs and making memories, it's back home.

– Day 30 Recipe –
PICARDY PANCAKES

Crêpes, or as we call them, pancakes, are common all over France, especially in Brittany. Also, galettes, which are similar but use buckwheat flour. I find that a savoury pancake is a great option for breakfast, lunch or even dinner, especially if you want something lighter to accommodate a dessert or a cheese plate afterwards. Fillings of course can be tailored to suit what you have, or your preferences. Here, I used bacon, mushrooms, and spinach.

Ingredients (serves 2)
Pancake Batter
- 12 tablespoons plain flour
- 210ml milk
- 1 large egg

Filling
- Splash of oil
- 4 rashers of bacon, chopped into small squares (*or 100g lardons*)
- 10 large mushrooms, sliced
- 4 handfuls of spinach
- Salt and pepper
- 4 tablespoons grated cheese

Method
Gently fry the bacon and mushrooms in the oil for a few minutes in a shallow frying pan, and season with salt and pepper as they cook. Add the spinach and allow it to wilt down.

Put the cooked bacon, mushrooms and spinach to one side in a bowl while you make the pancake batter. (I used the same pan for both the filling and then the pancakes.)

Beat the egg and milk together in a jug. Place the flour into a bowl, and slowly whisk in the egg and milk mixture to make a smooth batter.

Place the frying pan back on the heat and rub the pan with butter to grease.

Pour enough batter into the pan to just cover the base. Cook for a minute or so on each side, and then repeat for the second pancake. Wrap the cooked pancake in tinfoil to keep warm until both are cooked.

Then take each pancake in turn and lay on a plate to fill. Place some of the bacon, mushroom and spinach filling along the centre of each pancake and add a little cheese on the top. Fold over two sides of the pancake to encase the filling a little.

Carefully lift back into the pan and place on the heat for a minute to reheat slightly and serve! Repeat the procedure for the remaining pancake.

Everything can have drama if it's done right, even a pancake!

Julia Child

– Home Again –

REFLECTIONS

I **am back in the UK now** after my 30 days of motorhoming in Europe, and I am in reflective mood. If you have travelled this far with me, I thank you – it has been a fabulous journey, and a learning curve. I didn't really expect it to be a learning curve, as I thought I was well equipped both physically and mentally. Gosh, that sounds a bit dramatic, as if I have been on a space mission rather than a tootle into Europe, but anyway, that aside, I have taken lots out of the trip, and I think it stands me in better stead as my life's journey continues.

What did I learn then? Let me start at the beginning, where I set my intentions, and take it from there.

I wanted to be kinder to John. I get irritated very easily with my husband, and on this trip, as we were glued together more than we normally would be, I knew that there would be occasions when I would lose my cool. I didn't succeed entirely with my intention, and we had some difficult moments, but the good times far outweighed these. Overall, I think I can tick the kindness box, and what I did learn was that a partial success is better than none.

The same with living in the moment. I didn't hit 100 percent with this one, as being so busy and moving on and planning for each day sometimes took me outside the moment. However, the big win for me on this one was the taking of notes for my diary entries. Observing every small thing that I saw on each day that we travelled helped me to be more aware of where I was at that moment, and to appreciate the landscape and nature so much more. This trip has really shown me that keeping a journal is a good thing, and that helped me reflect on my daily adventures.

My third intention was to swim each day. Well, I think I need a medal, I did it! Although there were days when I didn't fancy going to the pool, each time I did I felt fabulous afterwards. I learned that setting an intention for this kind of thing really worked, as it was all under my own control, plus you never really regret doing something physical. If you think about it, how many people after, say, going for a walk, come back and wished they hadn't bothered?

One big thing this trip has taught me is that I can really get to grips with new things. For example, taking photographs. I must have taken thousands of pictures on this trip, all with my phone. At the beginning, the photos were OK, but I could see that they were improving every day, I was getting into it and looking all the time for the next great shot. It reinforced that story I tell people about me learning to bake, and all the crazy, extravagant things I can make now – had I never tried in the first place, I would never have known what talents lay hidden deep within me. I have taken most of the photographs in this book, bar the ones that John has taken of course!

I have been reflecting on the nuts and bolts of the trip too. In terms of the sites, we stayed on 14 in total. I got to wondering, which were my top three (discounting Château de l'Epivière as that has a special place in my heart anyway)? In no particular order, I think they were:

Ardèche
The site in the Ardèche. Why? There are so many reasons: it has such a dramatic landscape, we had a good pitch near the river, and it was also a trip down memory lane, as we had been before years ago. Last but not least, that fateful trip in the canoe was an unmissable experience and one I will never forget.

Tuscany
The site in Tuscany was another highlight. Its location atop a plateau overlooking the beautiful Tuscan landscape was amazing, and the campsite staff were all very amenable and jolly. I loved my cooking class where I made pasta from scratch, and it was great that the site offered the (very cheap) shuttle-bus service that allowed us to go on trips to Vinci and to Florence.

Venice
Finally, the site near Venice was also a favourite. It was big, but very attractive and lush, with an amazing supermarket full of goodies for me to ogle. The facilities were excellent, our pitch was big and only a minutes' walk from the sandy beach and very warm sea, but most of all we got to Venice from there with ease, a perfect mixture.

Speaking of Venice, that was my best day out during our trip and it also surprised me the most. I had expected Venice to be unbearably busy, but it wasn't on the day we visited. It was perfect – a magical mystery tour with all those nooks and crannies and the canals of course. Venice has such magnificent architecture too. I'd love to go back one day, and I'll definitely make sure to take a trip on a gondola next time.

Given how much time I spent on this trip in the swimming pool, I feel like I am now an expert! My tour of swimming pools was interesting in that there were so many different sizes, water temperatures, designs and so on. Although I was often a solo swimmer, there were times when the pool was busy with much splashing and jumping-in from youngsters (and oldsters too in some places). The best pool without doubt was that one in Tuscany, as it was an infinity pool looking over the romantic Tuscan landscape. However, there was a downside in that you had to wear bathing caps, not such a romantic look!

Another positive that has come out of this trip has been my increased body confidence. As the pool days went by, I realised I was getting less and less concerned with covering myself with either a towel or a sarong. Over the years, my weight has fluctuated, and when I am at the top end of my range (as I am now) I, like so many people, feel insecure and look to cover up. However, part way through the holiday I fancied a new swimming costume, and I bought a bright orange and rather revealing swimsuit. Once I put it on, the realisation came – quite out of the blue – that I really should love the skin I am in and embrace it.

That day, I posed for a photo in my swimsuit and felt free of any inhibition. It was an absolutely great feeling – we have one body and one life, so we shouldn't hide ourselves! On a similar note, I didn't open my make-up bag the entire time we were away. Perhaps once or twice, when I was rummaging in my handbag for a pen, I pulled out a lippie, and that prompted me to slick a bit on, but other than that, I wore no make-up at all. I was perfectly imperfect and loving it.

I think that brings me to the end of my reflections. This 30-day trip flew by. We visited so many lovely places and had some great new experiences. I must say that my diary and I are going from strength to strength, and we are in consultation now about our next adventure. It is in the early planning stages, but as they say, 'watch this space'.

USEFUL CONTACTS

If you have any enquiries, comments or questions please feel free to get in touch with me. I would love to hear from you!

Karen Wright
Karenwrightwakefield@hotmail.com
www.karenwrightbakes.co.uk

NOTE
The numbers below relate to the campsite locations on our route map, p6-7

Travel
The ferry company we used on this trip was DFDS. I often travel with them, as they still have a restaurant to enjoy a decent meal to start and end the trip. The motorhome was from Bailey of Bristol and our model was Adamo 69.4.

DFDS Ferries
www.dfds.com/en-gb

Bailey of Bristol
South Liberty Lane, Bristol BS3 2SS
www.baileyofbristol.co.uk

Campsites
Below is a list of all campsites that I stayed at during this trip, in chronological order. I am a member of the Caravan and Motorhome Club, and I booked them all through their European Campsites Brochure.

Caravan and Motorhome Club
East Grinstead House, East Grinstead, West Sussex RH19 1UA
www.caravanclub.co.uk

1 **Black Horse Farm Club Campsite**
385 Canterbury Rd, Densole, Folkestone CT18 7BG
www.caravanclub.co.uk/club-sites/england/
south-east-england/kent/black-horse-farm-club-campsite/

2 **La Belle Étoile**
1 Quai de Seine, 77000 La Rochette, France
www.campinglabelleetoile.com/en/

3 **Château de l'Epervière**
Rue du Château, 71240 Gigny-sur-Saône, France
www.les-castels.co.uk/camping/les-castels-chateau-de-lep-erviere

4 **Camping Nature Parc L'Ardéchois**
934 Route des Gorges, 07150 Vallon-Pont-d'Arc, France
www.ardechois-camping.com/en/

5 **Camping Sunêlia l'Hippocampe**
7 Rue de la Durance, 04290 Volonne, France
www.sunelia.com/en/france/provence-alpes-cote-d-azur/
alpes-de-haute-provence/volonne/l-hippocampe/

6 **Villaggio dei Fiori**
Via Tiro a Volo 3, Sanremo 18038, Italy
www.villaggiodeifiori.it/

7 **Camping Barco Reale**
Via Nardini 11, Lamporeccho (Pisoia) 51035, Italy
www.barcoreale.it/en/

8 **Camping Ca' Savio**
Via di Ca' Savio 77, Venice 30010, Italy
www.casavio.com/en/

9 **Camping Fontanelle**
Via de Magone 13, Moniga del Garda 25080, Italy
www.hghotels.com/de/property-item/camping-fontanelle/

10 **Camping Gemmi**
Briannenstrasse 8, Susten 3952, Switzerland
www.campgemmi.ch/

11 **Camping de l'Ill - Colmar**
1 Allée du camping, 68180 Horbourg-Wihr, France
www.campingdelill.fr/en/

12 **Camping Les Portes d'Alsace**
40 Rue de Père Lieberman, 67700 Saverne, France
www.vacances-seasonova.com/en/camping/camping-les-portes-dalsace-in-saverne-alsace/

13 **Camping Au Bord de L'Aisne**
14 Rue des Godins, 02190 Villeneuve-sur-Aisne, France
www.camping-aisne-picardie.fr/

14 **Camping La Bien Assise**
Av. de la Libération, 62340 Guînes, France
www.camping-la-bien-assise.com/en/

HANDY TRANSLATIONS

When you are out and about buying groceries in Italy and France well, anywhere really, you can usually identify things by sight – potatoes look like potatoes – but occasionally you may have to ask for things if you can't find what you're looking for. The following list covers most groceries used in the recipes in this book. Remember though, necessity is the mother of invention, and recipes evolve when alternative ingredients are used, so use what you like, or try something new. That can often be when the magic happens! Remember also, it is usually appreciated if you try to speak the language wherever you may be in the world, so just have a go and see what happens. You may come home with ingredients that you didn't ask for, but then you can just play 'ready, steady, cook'!

English	French	Italian
Herbs		
Basil	Basilic	Basilico
Coriander	Coriandre	Coriandolo
Parsley	Persil	Prezzemolo
Thyme	Thym	Timo
Vegetables		
Aubergine/eggplant	Aubergine	Melanzana
Capers	Capres	Capperi
Chilli	Piment	Peperoncino
Courgette/zucchini	Courgette	Zucchina
Garlic	Ail	Aglio
Leek	Poireau	Porro
Mushroom	Champignon	Fungo
Olive	Olive	Oliva
Onion	Oignon	Cipolla
Bell pepper	Poivron	Peperone
Tomato	Tomate	Pomodoro
Meat/fish		
Anchovies	Anchois	Acciughe
Beef burger	Steak haché	Hamburger
Chicken	Poulet	Pollo
Beef mince	Bœuf haché	Carne macinata
Sausage	Saucisse	Salsiccia
Sirloin steak	Faux filet	Lombata
Dairy and eggs		
Butter	Beurre	Burro
Cheese	Fromage	Formaggio
Cream	Crème	Crema
Eggs	Oeufs	Uova
Milk	Lait	Latte
Store-cupboard staples		
Bread	Pain	Pane
Flour	Farine	Farina
Oil	Huile	Olio
Pasta	Pâtes	Pasta
Rice	Riz	Riz
Sugar	Sucre	Zuchero

ACKNOWLEDGEMENTS

There are so many people that have helped and supported me during this book project, and I would like to express my appreciation to them all. First, all the people and souls who I mention in this book have left an imprint on me in a positive way at some time in my past, and I thank and remember them for it. I'd like to thank my new friend, my alter ego 'Diary', for listening to my daily ramblings and acting as a strong pair of emotional shoulders to lean on.

I thank my husband John for driving us everywhere so I could muse and watch the landscape and take notes for my book. I also thank him for his (at times begrudging) efforts as my photographer when I needed to be in a photo, and for his acceptance that most of his meals involved pasta and many of the other things on his 'don't really like' list. A big thank you goes to Sally sat-nav for her efforts getting us to our destination on each leg of the journey.

I'm grateful to Nikki Nichol and the Caravan and Motorhome Club for facilitating the trip, and to Bailey of Bristol for the loan of a cracking motorhome. Thanks to Sammy Faircloth for talking me through the self-publishing journey and inspiring me to take the plunge.

I'd like to thank all the people who helped with recipe-testing: Phil, Ronelia, Geoff, Dee, Janet, Kev, Russell, Keith, Susan, David, Jeremy and the Pennine Caravan Centre.

I'm also grateful for my friends Terry and Stephen and their daily messages of support, as well as my mum, Glenys, whose robust attitude to life and determined independence enables me to go on adventures. Also, thanks to my grandchildren, my brown-eyed girl Silke and my blue-eyed boy Nicu, who bring joy to my heart every day.

Lastly, many thanks go to my team: Steve Rendle, my project manager cum editor; Mark Case, my designer and brother from another mother, for putting together this stunning book; my daughters Kit and Vanessa for editing my ramblings, sifting through my photographs, and for their words of encouragement along the way. Between us, pulling together and giving where and what we can, we got this book to print. Thank you one and all – #gratitude.

Karen

HAPPY CAMPING: POSTCARDS FROM OUR TRIP...